Econor Crash - Course

How To Survive and Thrive

First Edition 2021

©Glen Carol

Contents

Introduction

In Order To Profit, You Have To Know What's Happening…

What Will Cause The Dominos To Fall?

How To Prepare.

Mindset - Existence vs Empire

Run Your Life Like A Business

Aim To Be Financially Independent ASAP

How To Potentially Profit From The Crash

Becoming Self Employed

Traits and Mindset

Time and Money Management

The Internet

How To Set Up An Online Business

Assets Vs Liabilities

Give Back

Conclusion

Introduction

Take a look at the world around you.

It is becoming increasingly easy to see what is coming.

Financial mania is everywhere.

Stocks, crypto coins, real estate.

Everywhere you turn there are "hot tips" and organized rallies to drive up asset prices.

A simple look at history, by anyone wise enough to do so, will highlight similarities of events past.

Major economic events that shook the world.

The symptoms around us are eerily similar to 2008, 1929, and various other points in history.

The majority of people refused to accept that the party would end.

That things were going to continue going up and the bubbles could only get bigger.

But, as we all know, the bubbles burst.

They burst, and they burst in a spectacular fashion.

So many people were "shocked" and countless people were financially devastated.

If you mentioned a crash before those historic events, the majority of people would laugh and dismiss such notions.

The same is true now.

Yet again.

People are in mania and think that the party will never end.

But it will.

Sooner, and more suddenly, than many people realize.

A lot of people are going to get financially crushed.

Some people are going to make an absolute fortune.

This is always the case in economic crashes across history.

Most people lose everything, simply because they were not paying attention in the majority of cases.

Crashes are almost always preceded by a period of hype and mania.

New "investors" are everywhere you turn and no one thinks the party will end.

But it always does.

In spectacular fashion.

By the time you have finished this book, you will likely agree with what I have said and will start making preparations to not only survive, but hopefully thrive.

Perhaps you will finish this book and disagree.

That is fine, and your decision.

But, just remember, if I am right…

You knew better and you knew ahead of time.

It is August 1st 2021 as I finish off this book ready for publication.

Time is running very low.

Very low indeed.

Read this book and make up your own mind about what you read in these pages.

Take what you will from it and use, modify, or discard points at your own discretion.

Because regardless of your final opinion, there are things in here that will get you thinking very seriously about the way the world is evolving around us.

It will also get you thinking about how you intend to profit from it.

Before you make any financial investments of any kind, you should always do your own research and seek professional advice.

Nothing in this book is intended to be, or should be considered, professional financial advice.

It is merely my opinion and this book is written to get you thinking about the concepts I present.

The world is soon to go through some major economic events.

You will have the information and then it is up to you to decide what course of action is best for you.

But remember.

In a crash, most people get financially crushed.

Some make absolute fortunes.

It's up to you to act in your own favor.

In Order To Profit, You Have To Know What's Happening…

As I write this, on August 1st, 2021, the economic markets are in a mania.

Many asset classes are volatile and are, or have been, at record highs.

With social media being at the center of many people's lives today, a day does not seem to pass without a crypto coin or a specific stock hashtag trending.

There have been organized pushes to drive up specific stocks or coins and the results have been spectacular to witness.

Cries of "too the moon" resound across the online world as waves of small investors organize themselves into buying frenzies in order to make money.

Granted. some of these investors have made money, but there have also been many that bought in at the top of the rallies only to see the price plummet as the early waves of investors sold off.

The term "bagholder" is now mainstream.

This has happened with both specific stocks and crypto coins.

These organized moves have drawn so much attention that financial regulators and institutions have been looking at the situation very closely.

But, as I type this, more rallies are being organized and the crowd seems to be optimistic that they can repeat their successes again and again.

Real Estate prices in many areas are surging, and again, many people are becoming involved as they see the potential for profits and do not want to miss out.

Make no mistake, we are in a mania, pretty much across the board.

If history is our teacher, then this is far from a good sign.

In fact, to the wise, it should be a huge warning sign.

Already experts are warning that the signs are looking very similar to 2008.

If we were to look further back in history, then we would see similarities to another era.

The 1920's.

The run-up to the great crash of 1929.

Some of you may be thinking that standpoint is overcautious.

Is it?

Let's take a quick look at some elements that today has in common with those eras.

In 2008, assets such as real estate were at record prices and it seemed that everyone you spoke to was a real estate investor or aiming to sell their home when it hit this or that price.

Everyone was talking about buying a property at one price, and selling it in a short time frame for a higher price.

"It's easy!"

"Everyone's doing it!"

"My friend/brother/neighbor made x amount last month"

"This won't end anytime soon. There's no way. The markets hot and going higher"

"My realtor said the price will easily hit x amount within 6 months."

"You are crazy if you don't get in on this. Everyone's making money. Don't miss out"

I'm sure you get the idea.

So many "hyped" people.

So many "investors"

I moved to Las Vegas in 2006 and I saw firsthand the mania in that city.

I also saw the fall out first hand when the crash happened and the real estate in Vegas was one of the worst-hit in the United States.

So many "shocked" people.

So many financially devastated people.

If you take the time to look into the 1929 crash, you will see very similar elements.

Everyone had a hot stock tip.

Everyone was an "investor"

Everyone was doing it.

You were "crazy" if you didn't get in on the action and would "miss out"

Then it crashed.

So many "shocked" people.

So many financially devastated people.

Look at today across the board.

Real Estate, stocks, and crypto coins.

See any of the same elements?

Isn't "everyone" doing it?

Are there plenty of "hot tips" floating around?

Have you heard stories of this or that person making x amount of money in a small time frame?

Are many people convinced that prices are going way higher and there's no end in sight?

Certain asset prices are "going to the moon" according to some "investors"

It all sounds very familiar…

The problem with a lot of these new "investors" is that they literally do not know what they are doing.

They have no idea what they are buying into.

They simply know that everyone else is buying in and making money, so they would be crazy to "miss out"

I have been watching various live streams on YouTube and other platforms as people trade live in front of viewers.

Some of the people in the chat feeds make very good points and display knowledge on investing.

But, swathes of them, ask questions and make comments that are quite frankly, alarming.

I have seen people say they bought x amount of this or that stock or coin at the previous market top and need it to hit that price again just to break even.

I have then seen people in comments give them advice such as,

"It's OK, just hold on. It will hit x amount easily. Just wait"

An example would be people who bought Bitcoin at $60k only to see it sink into the mid $30k range.

I have seen multiple people tell them to not worry and hold because it will hit $250k a coin soon enough.

But we are not in a mania.

No mania here.

Prices are "going to the moon"

Do you see my point?

There are certain stocks, you probably know which ones, with similar online chit-chat surrounding them.

Concerned people who bought in at the previous top price being told that the current drop is nothing to worry about because it is "going to the moon"

I have been investing somewhere in the region of a decade now.

I have seen all kinds of hype along the way.

This entire economic bubble is being inflated by it.

Hype and money printing.

Many experts are becoming very concerned about the amount of money printing currently taking place in the major world economies.

All of the old currencies are being printed into oblivion.

Do a Google search and look for recent articles from financial websites that are concerned about the rapidly increasing inflation caused by printing.

Now, when I say "printing" I don't mean literal printing of paper currency.

I mean mostly numbers on screens.

But I will use the term "printing" just as a blanket term to keep things simple.

Money is being conjured up left and right by governments for various aid packages, bailouts, and stimulus packages.

We are talking trillions.

Most of these governments are already trillions in debt and were borrowing money to keep things running before the outbreak.

So, after 2020 and the huge economic impact the outbreak had on businesses, employment, spending, etc, then surely tax revenue would have been significantly lower?

If government income is lower, and they were already borrowing when things were booming, then where has all this money turned up from?

Printing.

It's being created and pumped into the economy to keep things running and hopefully spur things back to normal.

Ok, great, you may be thinking.

But here's the key.

The more money they print, the less value, and therefore purchasing power, the currency has.

People are already noting that everyday goods, such as groceries, etc, are edging higher.

This is a sign of inflation.

A weakening in the purchasing power of the currency.

Devaluation.

Here is something to consider.

The "powers that be" have new digital currencies close to being introduced.

Take a moment to do a Google search and look into the following official digital currencies.

Digital Dollar

Digital Yuan

Digital Ruble

Digital Pound

Digital Euro

Digital Yen

I could go on and on with this list and cover most, if not all, of the world currencies.

The world is moving to digital currencies and sooner than the majority of people realize.

The information is on official pages, such as the Bank of England site, European Central Bank site, etc.

But the mainstream media is not yet really mentioning how close we are to this transition.

For example, the digital Yuan and Ruble are projected to go into mainstream use by the end of 2021.

Have you seen much talk about this on the news?

Any mention at all?

Consider this.

It is no secret that the West does not want to see the Eastern powers gain global economic dominance.

Especially China and Russia.

Although they may sit back for a short while to see what obstacles the digital Yuan and Ruble encounter at launch and how they resolve them, they will not want them to get a significant head start.

So, if they are launching at the end of 2021, would it be fair to say that we could potentially see the launch of a digital Dollar, Pound, Euro, and others in 2022?

I think it is very possible and let me tell you why I think this.

Firstly, as I said above, they are not going to want to let the Eastern powers get too far ahead in the new digital currency global economy.

Earlier I mentioned the concerns about money printing.

This can, and is, leading to inflation.

For a moment, I'm going to assume you know nothing about how inflation affects an economy and therefore society.

Inflation is a complex topic, but let's just take a moment to realize that the more money that is in circulation, the less it is worth.

So, new money in circulation is slowly chipping away at the purchasing power of the savings you, or anyone else, may have that is denominated in dollars.

If milk and other goods rise in price by 3% then you need to have your savings in a savings account that pays you 3% after any capital gains taxes and account fees just to break even as far as inflation.

So, the more money that gets put into circulation, then the higher inflation goes on goods and services.

You may not care about milk, bread, etc going up a few cents.

But when you put that inflation across your weekly, and especially yearly, living expenses, it really starts to show up.

The more money they print, the less value, and therefore purchasing power, the currency has.

People are already noting that everyday goods, such as groceries, etc, are edging higher.

This is a sign of inflation.

A weakening in the purchasing power of the currency.

Devaluation.

Here is something else to consider.

The "powers that be" have new digital currencies close to being introduced.

The old currencies are being devalued by printing.

What if, in order for the new digital currencies to be rolled out with a fresh start and welcomed with open arms by the public, the old currencies had to "die", so to speak.

To become basically worthless, or at least in comparison to the new digital currencies.

Do you think that if we suffered some serious inflation problems and people were struggling to make ends meet as the old currencies became increasingly worthless, that people would welcome a solution?

That full transition to the new digital currencies may become a very desirable necessity?

A necessity that had to happen suddenly and quickly?

Perhaps on the back of a major economic crash?

One similar to 2008 or even 1929?

Do you see where I am heading with this?

This current mania cannot continue and will not continue.

It will end.

If history is our teacher, it will end very badly.

The old currencies will be in serious trouble.

Devalued.

The stage will be set for a severe need for economic change.

New official digital currencies will be that change.

I am not the only one who sees this coming.

If you look into the news you will find that recently Russia began dumping its dollar-dominated assets.

Why do you think this is?

Do you think they are concerned about the ongoing devaluation of the dollar and are trying to get out while there is still time?

Do you think they can see what is coming?

They are not alone.

China has been incrementally moving away from dollar-based assets for a while.

Trillions worth.

Is it a coincidence that these two powers are also the closest to launching their digital currencies?

Perhaps.

But I don't think so, and neither do an increasing number of other people.

The Western powers are busily devaluing their currencies and are working on getting their digital currencies ready to launch.

The Eastern powers are dumping their Western denominated assets and getting ready to launch their digital currencies.

What do you think is coming?

Combine this with the current mania in stocks, crypto, real estate, and other asset classes.

We are looking at a potential perfect storm.

A storm that will rock the global economic system.

That will bring in a new digital economy.

Here is something else the vast majority of the public are not aware of.

Back in September of 2019, there was trouble in the Repo market.

The Repo market is for interbank lending.

The basic concept is this.

When you deposit money in the bank, let's say $10k, the bank is required to hold a certain amount in reserve in order to cover withdrawals.

Typically, it is around 10%, but it varies.

So, if you put $10k in the bank, they borrow $9k out for loans and investments.

Mortgages and such.

Now, this is not to say you can't get the full $10k if you want it.

They will juggle numbers and you will have your $10k upon request.

The key is, the banks know how much they typically have deposited and withdrawn on certain days of the year.

Typically.

For example, a lot of people have their paychecks deposited in their accounts on the 1st of the month, etc.

They have years of people's account history to know that people usually have this debited on that day, this bill goes on another, etc.

The numbers are not going to fluctuate as wildly as you may think.

At least when you are playing with bank numbers.

Jim may suddenly decide to withdrawal $20k one day for a purchase, but typically, he doesn't.

When you are playing with bank numbers involving millions and billions, $20k is a drop in the ocean as far as a fluctuation.

Even if there's a hundred "Jims" per day.

This is known as fractional reserve banking.

So, if there is some wild fluctuations and the bank is not certain that they will have the money to cover the coming few day's withdrawals etc, they will go to the repo market.

The market allows bank A to borrow from bank B

Bank B will usually charge x amount of interest for the 3 days.

The money is borrowed and paid back, and that's that.

The bank's customers get their withdrawals with no hassle and no one is any the wiser nor is any harm done.

It's a good system in my opinion.

However.

In September of 2019, the Repo market had "issues"

There is a government bailout fund that covers the repo market in the event of any "issues"

Issues such as bank B not willing, or able, to borrow bank A money or charging a higher than normal interest rate because they see a risk in borrowing to Bank A for some reason.

In such a scenario, Bank A can turn to the bail-out fund and borrow the money from there.

It is paid back, and no one is none the wiser, and all is well.

However, there is information online that,

In September 2019, the bail-out fund was utilized several times.

In October 2019, the fund was used a lot.

In November 2019, the fund was used, shall we say, heavily.

There were issues with people getting money out of their accounts.

"Technical difficulties" with online banking systems etc.

I'm not giving numbers because I want you to research for yourself, and to be fair, they vary from source to source, so I can't say "it was this much" with any degree of certainty.

Anything I say in this book you should research.

I only put what I have researched.

So if I write it, you can go and research it for yourself and draw your own conclusions.

But be aware of this and look into it for yourself.

The repo market has been, shall we say, interesting, again back in May 2021.

This trend is continuing now in June 2021.

Do your research and see what conclusions you draw from this.

My conclusion is that the economic pot is bubbling.

How long do we have until it comes to a boil?

Here is where we look at aspects we all need to be cautious of.

If you are currently invested, or aiming to invest, in crypto coins, stocks, bonds, or even real estate, then you really need to start to pay attention to what is happening.

I will start with a quick story from history.

Joseph Patrick Kennedy, JFK's father, was getting his shoes shined back in 1929.

The shoeshine guy started giving him hot stock tips.

Mr. Kennedy knew then that it was time to get out of the market.

He did, it crashed, and he bought back in at the bottom and made millions.

You may have worked out the moral of the story for yourself, but let me put it into my own words.

He realized that when you have everyone and their dog throwing stock tips around, you are in a bull market that is guided by rumors and sheer numbers of people piling into assets based upon those rumors.

It's a mania.

The prices are being driven by hype and not fundamentals.

A company can be doing badly, but if enough people pile into the stock, it will rise in value.

More people see these gains and want to get in on the action.

Up and up it goes.

Now, I'm sure you are aware of the great crash of 1929 and the subsequent great depression?

How masses of people who had been flying high were financially crushed within days.

Where were the rumors and tips that could have saved them?

Where were the shoeshine boy's pearls of financial wisdom?

The people who knew what they were doing had already got out and sat back with a pile of cash waiting for the crash ready to buy up all the tanked stocks at cut-rate prices.

Do you see the same symptoms?

Isn't everyone suddenly an investing whizz?

Is social media full of trending hashtags such as #tothemoon and organized stock buying days, such as what happened with GameStop?

Do you think this can go on forever?

How many people got stung by the GameStop scenario?

Yes, people made money.

But how many got burnt by getting in late on the back of the hype?

Plenty.

I'm not for one minute saying get out of stocks now, but I am saying we are not on a good economic trajectory.

If you can make money now before things tip, then great.

Make hay while the sun shines.

But bear in mind what I have said so far.

All the symptoms are there.

Back in January 2017 Bitcoin was at around $900.

Hype, rumors, and mania started later that year.

In December 2017 it hit around $20k.

By February 2018 it had fallen to the $6k range.

The rise and fall were based on what?

Rumors, hype, and mania.

People surging in and out based on those factors.

Many people made money, but plentiful were the stories of people who had got in at the top and were trapped unless they took significant losses by selling.

As the rise occurred, there were plenty of rumors and tips spreading like wildfire.

"Bitcoins going to the moon!"

"Get in now, don't miss out!"

"So and So said it will hit at least $100k!"

Based on what?

Enough people piling in on the back of rumors and hashtags?

Sound familiar?

Between crypto and stocks, we are in a mania.

Markets of all kinds are full of shoeshine investors.

How do you think this is going to end?

Rest assured, all markets experience boom and bust cycles.

It's baked into the cake.

It's inescapable.

Look at 2008 and the housing crash, let alone the rest of the economic chaos.

Everyone was piling into real estate.

I buy it for $300k and I sell it at $400k, it's easy!

Then the $400k buyer plans to sell it at $500k, it's easy!

We all saw how that mania turned out.

Everyone was a real estate expert.

It was going up and up in this area or that.

"Get in or miss out!"

Sound familiar?

Because it should.

We are in a mania across the board right now.

Just like in the roaring twenties and just like in the run-up to 2008.

Ever heard of the dot-com bust in the '90s?

Similar tale.

Or how about the Black Monday stock crash in the 80s?

Google research into booms and busts and economic cycles, there are plenty of examples from history to chew on.

All have something in common though.

Mania-induced highs.

If you are invested in crypto coins, I would like you to consider the following points.

China slammed the price of cryptos when they announced their ban back in May 2021.

Investors were shocked as they saw the prices plummet.

Then came the news of new I.R.S. regulations for taxation purposes.

Price was hit again.

But consider this.

When the official digital currencies are past the testing stage and are accepted as part of daily life, they will almost certainly have ledgers built in to track the spending of the currency for taxation purposes and also to prevent any criminal activity.

Not a bad thing in my opinion at all.

But, let that sink in.

Now, do you think that these next points are fair assumptions?

1. They are not going to want people using anonymous crypto coins to do transactions and avoid their new system.
2. They are not going to want such coins in existence that allow nefarious groups to do exactly that.

There have already been rumblings in the mainstream news about Crypto being used for nefarious purposes.

Could the path be being laid for an outright ban, either before, or just after the introduction of the new digital currencies?

Will there be a warning, or will it happen overnight to prevent nefarious groups from moving their money to another haven?

Will the "hashtaggers" give a warning to all their followers ahead of time?

Or will a lot of people suddenly find themselves with all their gains frozen or even dissolved as Bitcoin is not able to be used and therefore valued at zero?

Think it can't happen?

I simply say, China ban.

I called potential incoming government crypto bans on one of my blogs on May 1st 2021.

People thought I was nuts.

Especially the hashtagger crowd.

I was proven to be correct on May 18th.

If you are invested in crypto coins, then you really need to monitor on a regular basis how close the official digital currencies are moving along to launch.

Because there will be no warning from the hashtagger crowd as May 18th proved.

They only want to hear about #toothemoon and how they will all be millionaires from dogecoin.

They are completely swept up in the mania and it will not end well for many, if not most, of them.

Something I suspect will make matters worse for crypto investors is the inflation and what will happen when the crash hits.

Mark my words, when the time comes and the stock markets are crashing and the old currencies are in serious trouble, the hashtaggers will start pushing crypto coins as a safe haven.

The prices will surge.

You may see the $100k+ Bitcoin they all tout.

But here is the kicker.

If people are pumping the price up by piling in with the old inflated currencies.

Do you think the "powers that be" will want that inflation spilling back out into the fresh new currencies?

Spoiling their fresh start?

The great reset?

Or do you think they may just put in a ban preventing financial institutions from accepting withdrawal from trading platforms etc?

Not like it hasn't been done before…

I'm looking at you China.

Now you could say, "well, I'll look into trading out into other coins that can be converted into the new currency. Ones that don't use anonymous ledgers or become too inflated"

Voila.

Now you are starting to see why I wrote this book.

I'm trying to help people become aware ahead of time and plan accordingly.

I may have taken a while to get to this point, but I really wanted you to see how listening to these "hashtaggers" and following the herd is going to absolutely crush some people in the future.

I hesitate to say, potentially near future.

I hope my readers at least consider what I am saying, do their own research, and plan based on what they decide.

The number of people I saw on social media absolutely crushed and in a panic as they saw their portfolios plummet when China made their moves was astounding.

The argument some "hashtaggers" have made is "Bitcoin will get to $100k, $200k, whatever, but it'll take time. Several years"

As I said earlier, China is planning to roll out into mainstream public use at the end of 2021.

The other major countries are field testing and will not want to let them have a huge head start.

Granted they may hold back a short period just to see what mistakes or obstacles China may encounter as they implement, but they are not going to let them have "years" of a head start.

So, with that said, I think we should consider the possibility that the new digital Dollar, Pound, Euro, etc will be rolled out into public use in perhaps 2022.

Twelve months perhaps.

Maybe a bit longer, maybe a bit less.

Could I be wrong?

Absolutely.

But is what I am saying feasible?

I think so.

In fact, I'm planning around it.

If I'm off on my estimate, no worries, I have more time to prepare and adapt as I go.

If I'm right, I will be well ahead of the "hashtaggers" and their flock.

My question to you is,

"Do you think I am potentially right based on what I have said?"

We are all fully aware of the rivalry between East and West.

Chinas out in front in their testing and Russia is making headway.

Do you think the West is going to sit on their laurels and let their arch-rivals get a head start into the new digital-based global economy?

Honestly?

Do you think the rest of the world is going to sit back and simply watch.

Japan, for example?

I think we are on the cusp of a global transfer to a digital currency-based economy.

A lot closer than most people realize.

I also think that the transition will be sudden and rapid.

Considering the general public's current skepticism towards digital currencies, thanks to the recent Bitcoin debacle, I don't think most countries have time to woo them to a transition.

I think it will be presented as a desirable necessity.

That something will unfold that will cause a severe need to transfer over to the new digital system, and rapidly.

And, for our own good, of course…

I think we could be on new digital currencies by some time in 2022 and the old currencies will either be gone or close to phased out.

The combination of inflation and the race to digital being lead by China will force the West and the rest of the world to act.

The public is not ready yet, so it will be born out of desirable necessity rather than a slow wooing of the public.

In the next section, I will tell you what I think could produce this scenario of "desirable necessity"

What Will Cause The Dominos To Fall?

Here is pure speculation on my part.

I claim no different.

I am not for one moment saying, "this is what will happen"

I'm presenting a scenario based on what I think and why.

It is not what I KNOW and set in stone.

I will adapt my stance as I go on my blog and also adapt my personal financial moves in the same way.

Day by day.

But, let's see what COULD happen.

A scenario, if you will.

One to illustrate my concepts and to get you thinking for yourself on the matter.

Bear with me on this, and be sure to do your own research and come to your own conclusions.

Back in September of 2019, there was trouble in the Repo market, as I said earlier.

Next on the menu, was, of course, the outbreak.

We all saw what that did to the global economy.

Many people lost their jobs and numerous businesses closed for good.

Take a moment to consider what that did to both government income via tax collection and government expenditure via people applying for aid and various bailouts and stimulus packages.

You know, those governments that are carrying heavy debt loads...

Yet, through all of this, the stock markets raged to historic highs and are still flying high as I type this.

So, bear these points in mind as we go.

A shaky repo market just before the outbreak.

The outbreak hit the global economy hard.

Heavily indebted governments handing out conjured money left and right.

Stock markets at historic highs, based mainly on a flood of investors' money rather than actual company performance in a lot of cases.

Think "GameStop"

They are not unique or the sole darlings of "hashtaggers" put it that way.

Crypto volatility due to both "hashtaggers" and government bans and regulations.

Official digital currencies being developed and field-tested.

A lot of talk in the media of new variants of the virus and possibly new outbreaks.

OK, got them in mind?

Then let's proceed.

Here is what I think will happen.

Potentially.

A scenario, if you will.

China is currently out in front as far as being ready to implement its digital currency into mainstream use.

Other major economies, mainly the U.S., UK, Eurozone, and Russia, are all playing catch up.

At least that seems to be the case at this point.

The markets are at record highs and cryptos, despite their volatility, are still in a mania and are most likely going to start to recover in price.

Inflation of the old currencies is becoming an issue.

There are rumblings in the repo market again.

A lot of places are easing their lockdown policies and even removing compulsory mask policies.

Japan is currently having issues with a spike in infections, but we will keep this as a noted variable for now.

(I wish them all the best by the way. Japan is awesome in my opinion)

I think it may play out like this.

The hype and mania will continue over the summer months.

Come Flu season, October or thereabouts, a new variant will emerge.

It will trigger another lockdown.

Due to policies being relaxed over the 2021 summer it will be widespread, and most likely global, before lockdown is enacted.

I think most likely the lockdown will be announced in October and the reason given will be that policies were relaxed far too early and that not enough people were vaccinated.

Even if it is not global, regions will lock down borders to prevent spread from other regions.

This will slam the global economy.

Markets will crash and people will look for alternatives, i.e. Crypto such as Bitcoin.

A panic will kick in.

Governments will print like crazy to prop up the economy and will be faced with conjuring up money for not only bailouts for industries, but also further stimulus payments as the people lose their jobs as businesses close or reduce staff due to lockdown.

Meanwhile, China will introduce its digital currency into the mainstream and dump its remaining dollar assets due to the depreciation caused by the overprinting.

They will stabilize and be a shining example as their economy rides the global storm and most other places suffer.

The West will be printing money causing massive inflation and banks will have issues as deposits plummet and reserves tumble due to larger than normal withdrawals.

This will be due to people losing their incomes and also people having to withdraw more as inflation causes surges in the price of everyday goods.

I would not be surprised if capital controls are enacted and daily or weekly withdrawal limits are imposed.

Scarcity due to reduced production may also be an issue as manufacturers are closed for lockdown and also border controls are tightened for imports and exports.

We have seen this before, so it's not a mental leap of faith to see this panning out.

Remember empty supermarket shelves and not a toilet roll to be found, around 12 months ago?

It happened pretty much overnight.

As the situation worsens, and people see Bitcoin and co surging, the "hashtaggers" will start touting Bitcoin and co as the hedge against inflation and an alternative to the rapidly declining old currencies.

The governments with the old traditional currencies have a choice.

Keep printing and hope for the best as China surges forward with its digital Yuan.

Or.

Release their new digital currencies to replace the old ones.

Justification?

Multiple fronts.

"We can stabilize everything economically if we do a currency reset and go to digital"

"They work, look at China"

"We need to eliminate paper cash to cool inflation" or "Paper money carries the virus and is aiding the spread"

Removing the paper money supply will not be anywhere enough.

"If we move to this new digital currency at x conversion rate we can stabilize and look to getting back towards normality"

As people lose their jobs, crime and unrest surges due to economic frustrations, and everyday goods become scarce due to lockdowns or wildly expensive due to inflation, people will agree to this "desirable necessity"

Digital currency is introduced at a rate.

Who knows, the rate at this point?

10 old dollars for 1 new digital?

20 to 1?

50 to 1 if inflation is that crazy at that point?

Pure speculation at this point, but it sure as hell will not be 1 to 1.

Governments will put a block on financial institutions accepting withdrawals from crypto trading platforms to ensure that the inflation from them doesn't spill into new currencies.

Even if the rate is 20 to 1, and "too the moon" Bitcoin is $100k or more, they are not going to let millions of coins be cashed out and allow all that inflation to surge back into the new coins.

Besides, who are they going to sell to and in what?

Everyone will be rushing to the doors to sell, the price will plummet, and all anyone will be offering, in the highly unlikely event there are buyers, will be old currency at that point.

No one is going to be putting new digital currency into Bitcoin and most likely won't be able to transfer from their bank to the exchange anyway.

Things will start to stabilize, and Bitcoin and co will be worthless.

The final nail in the coffin of Bitcoin, in any event, will most likely be the following.

To prevent tax evasion and the nefarious movement of money for criminal groups and the like, crypto coins will be banned and only open ledger coins, at best, will be allowed.

Maybe.

Think that's a nuts scenario?

How about, Bitcoin to the $300k moon?

Stock markets never crashing?

Inflation via government printing never debasing the old currencies and killing the purchasing power affecting swathes of the lower-income population?

A flu-based virus never evolving into a stronger strain and causing another lockdown?

The West sitting back and allowing China and Russia to get a head start in the new digital currency age?

And the current mania party never ends?

Are you sure which one sounds nuts?

I mean, really sure?

I rest my case.

You may think that this all sounds like a bit of a stretch or a perfect storm.

Let's look at it this way.

As you celebrated the new year on Dec 31st 2019 did you have any notion that the world would be in complete lockdown a few months later?

Did you think that you would see empty store shelves and everyone forced to wear masks?

There was not even a sniff of evidence that it would be the case.

Yet it came to pass.'

Everything I have mentioned, I have told you to Google and do your own research.

Look at it this way.

Constantly printing money is not going to end well.

The West is not going to want China to get too far out in front with its digital implementation.

They are already planning to launch their own, otherwise, they would not be developing and testing them.

With all the talk of new strains emerging, relaxed policies allowing people to gather in public again, and flu season months away, a new strain taking hold is very possible.

The global economy simply cannot take another lockdown so soon.

There is a mania in most asset classes, crypto, stocks, etc.

Any one of these can cause a huge economic event.

We have all of them boiling at the same time, and all have the ability to trigger others in the chain.

As I said all through this book so far, you can do your own Google research on the things I have said.

You should do this and come to your own conclusions.

But I ask you to consider this.

Do you really think that the above points I have made, are completely out of the realm of possibility?

Do you think you will get any kind of "heads up" from the "hashtaggers" or that the "powers that be" will give any advance warning of bans?

I'm writing this book because I am doing what I can to get people to avoid potential disaster.

If I'm wrong, then good for all.

I'll still be just as fine as everyone else in that scenario.

If I'm right, then, I'll be fine because I saw it all coming, or at least kept track of key information as it unfolds.

So will anyone who at least considers what I have said and looks into these points further.

Will you be able to say the same?

Or are you going to rely on trending hashtags?

Because I assure you, one way or the other, this system is ready to come down to make way for the new digital currencies.

All the signs are there.

I'm not the only person who thinks this way.

It is not some half-baked conspiracy theory or "hashtagger" fluff.

There are plenty of financial experts who are very concerned about the trajectory we are on and the various potential tipping points taking position before us.

If you do think it's all a load of nonsense or overblown fear-mongering, then I wish you all the best.

But I will say this.

I'm not positioning myself as some kind of expert or trying to become some kind of financial seer.

I'm simply trying to get at least some people to see what is happening.

Because, make no mistake, those new digital currencies are coming.

Not "if", but "when", is the key.

I said, I doubt it will be a smooth transition and I suspect the "hashtaggers" and co are going to be caught completely off-guard and end up losing a lot of money.

If you do choose to ignore what I have said and carry on chasing hashtags, just remember, you knew better and you knew in advance.

Learn from the fall you take, and I wish you all the best.

Hopefully, I'm wrong.

But, we shall see.

Let's look at how you can prepare and potentially profit from this situation.

Before I go into this section I am going to make some things very clear.

None of what I say is intended or to be considered as expert or professional financial or investing advice.

I'm not a licensed financial professional and have never claimed to be so.

What I write here are merely suggestions of topics to get you inspired to do your own research and due diligence.

I am not going to recommend specific stocks or any other financial assets.

I am going to give my opinion on topics I think are worth researching.

It is not intended to be a financial blueprint or any kind of guarantee of profit.

Read this section and then go off and do your own research before putting a single penny into any financial venture or instrument, and do so under your own volition.

As always, some things you may agree with and some you may not.

My aim is to get you thinking.

I will start with basic day-to-day measures you can consider taking.

This is not some wild prepper talk, simply common sense things to consider.

After we have addressed these basic ideas then we will look at how to get into position to potentially profit from the crash.

How To Prepare.

In this section, we are going to look at where you are now and how you can prepare and be in the best position you can for when the crash starts.

Self-Assessment

In this section, we are going to look at various aspects of your current situation.

In order to know how to survive, and potentially thrive, in the coming economic environment, you have to know where you currently stand and how you got here.

Personal Finances.

The first thing that everyone needs to address is the current state of their personal finances and to put in the infrastructure to get into a better position.

I will break it down into easy step-by-step sections for you to consider and implement as you see fit.

This is designed to encourage you to address, assess, and take action with your current financial situation.

This self-assessment is going to drag you into reality, whether you like it or not. At the end of it, three things are possible, and one is guaranteed.

You will either be happy, content, or feeling aggravated.

But I will guarantee you this.

You will be staring reality firmly in the face.

If you do not like what you see, then it is up to you to fix it.

No one is going to do it for you.

This is all on you.

You will need the following things.

Pen and paper

Calculator

All of your bank account and credit card statements (Just log in online and have your last few months statement available for you to view)

Step 1

The first thing you need to do is note down exactly how much money you have around you today.

Your actual money on hand in your personal checking and savings accounts.

Step 2

Note down all of your monthly expenses such as rent, utility bills, and car loans.

Leave your credit card payments at this point.

Just note down what fixed payments you have going out each month.

Step 3

Note down your current credit card balance and minimum payment amount next to each one.

Step 4

Note down the last few income payments you received.

For most people, this is their wage deposit each time they get paid. If you have regular payments coming in from other sources (Fixed, not random money turning up) then include those.

Step 5

Go through all of your random spending and note it all down.

Everything from clothes, online shopping, gas for your car, groceries, beer, pet food, etc.

Whatever is not a fixed monthly bill taken from your account.

If you tend to withdraw cash for these purchases, then simply note all of your withdrawals.

Step 6

Go through these amounts and divide them into two separate groups.

Essential spending and non-essential.

Item by item.

For example, groceries are essential spending and beer is non-essential spending.

Step 7

Now, take a look at how much money you have wasted recently on non-essential items.

(Notice I said "Wasted" and not "Spent")

Step 8

Now break everything into the following groups with a total next to each one.

Checking Account Balance.

Savings Account Balance.

Monthly Bill Outgoings.

Credit Card Balances and Minimum Payments due.

Typical Income Amounts

Essential Spending

Non – Essential Spending

In front of you is your current financial reality.

This is where you stand.

For some, the picture might be great, or at least comfortable.

For others, it may cause them to hold their head in their hands in dismay.

In any case, it is what it is.

It's your financial reality whether you like it or not.

I'm not being harsh.

I'm simply trying to get you to grab this reality by the throat and take control of it instead of it controlling you.

The first step of treating any problem is knowing its causes.

You have to know why your finances look the way they do.

The good, bad, and ugly aspects of your financial life.

Ask yourself the following questions.

Do you have a healthy amount of reserve cash in your checking and savings accounts?

How long will they last if your typical monthly income stops and you are forced to use them for your monthly bills, credit card payments, and essential spending?

How much money have you wasted on non-essential spending recently?

Are you happy with what you see in front of you?

Are you willing to make changes or are you just going to close this book and pretend you never did this exercise?

Be honest with yourself because I will never know your answers.

Knowing where you stand in life is a great place to start plotting your course forwards.

Spending Discipline

The first thing you are going to have to do in order to adapt to this new world is to develop spending discipline.

We all like to treat ourselves and sometimes spoil others.

None of us want to live life pinching every penny and not enjoying ourselves.

But, if you look at your current totals and feel sick when you see those numbers, then you need to ask yourself what is more important in life.

"Being able to survive and pay your bills if you lose your job due to a future lockdown or layoff"

Or

"Living life in the moment and not worrying about next month"

If you chose the second option, then you have just found a problem in your financial mindset.

Your priorities and self-discipline are not in your own best interests.

In fact, they are actively harming your financial security.

If you are usually disciplined with your spending and have just hit hard times due to the economic impact of the lockdown, then my heart goes out to you.

If you were doing OK, but were spending money as fast as it came in before the lockdown due to pure lack of discipline.

In other words, you could have built up a reserve but chose to just blow your money each check and not worry about any bumps in the road.

Well, ask yourself this.

Was it worth it and how do you feel about it now?

Do you wish you could go back and act responsibly instead?

Well, sorry to say, you cannot, and all you can do is accept today and build onwards for tomorrow.

I know this sounds harsh, but it is time to financially mature and take control of your life.

Learn your lesson and swear to yourself that you will act responsibly from here on in.

Not get yourself to a comfortable position and then start the balancing act again.

Evolve here and now.

You are not doing this for me or making me any promises.

You are doing this for yourself and will have to keep yourself accountable.

Don't worry, we are going to look at how you can get all of this in order.

The first thing everyone needs to do at this point is to cut out all the non-essential spending until everything else is in position.

In the next section, we are going to look at how you can get money together to survive the coming months and to start building a reserve to be prepared for problems in the economy.

I know this section has been hard for some of you, but rest assured, ignoring it will not solve it.

Overall Financial Discipline.

In this section, we are going to look at how to develop financial discipline and correct your finances.

From here on in, you are going to have to exercise financial discipline.

We all are.

I don't care if you are sitting comfortably finance-wise, or on the edge of financial ruin.

The world is evolving, and we all need to adapt to this new environment if we expect to survive and thrive in the future.

It is a time of Economic Darwinism.

The world will not right itself overnight from the effects of this collapse.

As I write this, many parts of the globe are still at various levels of infection rate.

Things are looking precarious again at this point, and a return to some of the old policies, such as wearing masks, have been occurring in various regions.

Even though they have lifted lockdowns in many places across the globe, the economic ramifications of the previous lockdown are still unfolding.

If you are paying attention to the current economic reality for the average person, then you will be witnessing the true economic trajectory of this situation.

Inflation is starting to show up on everyday goods such as groceries and at the gas pump.

People are starting to feel the impact of the money printing and "Inflation" was even trending as a hashtag on social media a week or so ago.

When the crash occurs, millions will have lost their jobs, and many businesses will have either gone under or be in trouble.

I'm sure that after the new lockdowns lift, and less people are able to spend due to losing their job, more businesses will be suffering from the lower revenue, and more people will be laid off.

This will only compound the problem and lead to even more layoffs and even more failing businesses.

So, the cycle goes.

I also expect to see a lot of problems in the real estate sectors, both commercial and residential, as fewer people and businesses can pay their rent or mortgages.

In an environment such as this, do you really think you should just be spending as normal?

Leave caution to the wind?

No, of course not.

Your next task is actually quite simple.

Cut out your non-essential spending and trim back on your essential spending as best you can.

Non-essential spending is easy enough to sort out.

Stop buying things you do not need.

I don't care if you have a sweet tooth and buy a chocolate bar every day, or if it's that you just had to buy your cat that cute new coat.

Things are going to get tight economically and bills are more important than your sweet tooth or how many likes your cat gets on social media.

Stop your needless spending now.

Not tomorrow or after the weekend.

Now.

This minute.

For your own good.

I'm also going to jump ahead a little here as far as topics in this book.

If you follow through this book, you will find out how to potentially make a lot of money during this period and in the future.

But this is not going to happen if you do not have financial discipline.

The basics have to be set in place.

A fool and his money are easily parted.

It's no good having money if you do not have discipline.

Start now.

As far as essential spending, if possible, try to trim it back.

I understand that people need to buy groceries to live, but do you really need that box of cookies and six-pack of beer?

Go through your essential spending and see if there is anything you can trim back.

Again, if it is an essential purchase, then keep it, but see if you can maybe scale it back.

As crazy as it sounds, if you are used to having large portions of food, try to cut them back to make your food last longer.

Each time you run out of food and go shopping, it is more money spent.

Again, I'm not saying starve yourself.

I'm simply saying stretch things out a little in order to make your money stretch the same way.

Spending discipline is basically composed of two things.

Reducing and eliminating needless spending.

Only spending on things that are beneficial.

Later in the book, we will look at purchasing things such as assets instead of liabilities.

If you can't control your spending impulses with regards to simple things such as chocolate bars, then do not expect to make good purchases with larger amounts of money.

Balancing the books.

Now we have addressed financial discipline, then we should look at balancing the books as far as your financial situation.

Now, this is going to have to be adapted by yourself for your own personal financial situation.

The overall concepts are key to this and can be applied to anyone with some fine-tuning by the individual.

You have your typical income and outgoings in front of you and have addressed reducing your needless spending etc.

I'm going to assume that you still have a job, and therefore income, at this point.

If you do not, still read this and be ready to use these techniques when you replace your income.

The next thing you need to do is note down a total of all your typical monthly expenses into a "Basic Outgoings Total"

Add together your "Monthly Bill Outgoings", "Credit Card Minimum Payments Due", and "Essential Spending" totals to get one number.

This is the exact minimum you will need in the bank each month just to survive.

Compare this now to your current total of "Checking Account Balance" + "Savings Account Balance"

Add them together to get one number.

This is what you currently have in reserve to survive and then compare that number to the monthly spending total you just calculated.

How long do you have?

Six months?

A year?

A month?

This again is your financial reality.

Now take a look at how much non-essential spending you have eliminated by exercising spending discipline from here on in.

Has it covered a portion of your future bills?

Is it better to have that money in the bank as a reserve or better to have "Likes" on your cat's coat selfie?

See my point?

Don't forget what I mentioned earlier about the conversion rate and the transition to the new digital currencies.

We simply do not know what that rate will be.

I will address money in the bank and cash on hand now as we go forward.

Cash on Hand

As it stands currently, there are no issues with people accessing their bank funds that I am aware of.

During the last lockdown, most bank branches were closed, but ATMs were still functioning, and online banking was up and running.

But, it can be wise to have some cash around your home just so you can go out and grab essentials as and when you need them if we do have an economic event.

As we have all witnessed, water and cleaning supplies were cleared out in record time leaving empty shelves across the world.

Now, most people simply paid in cash or swiped their card to pay.

But, I would bet money that there were people who live paycheck to paycheck who were waiting for a deposit to land in their account before they could go shopping.

Would they have not been better off having at least a little bit of cash tucked away at home for emergencies?

Not a mattress full of cash, just enough to load up on a week's worth of supplies or at least until their deposit cleared.

I wonder how they got on when they had to wait for the deposit and ended up staring at empty shelves because they were later than the masses?

I do not know anyone who endured this, but I'm confident that more than one or two people did, put it that way.

I saw a few people in my area wandering around with an almost empty cart staring at the empty water aisles with concerned looks on their faces.

From here on in, I suggest that no matter what happens, you should keep enough cash on hand to buy things should a new lockdown or economic event occur and supermarket supplies endure the same panic-induced shortages.

With some people and businesses currently running low on money, we may have a situation that is known as a "Liquidity crisis"

This is where there is not enough money in the banks to keep things running correctly.

Banks keep a percentage of their total deposits on hand to cover any withdrawals, as I mentioned earlier.

I'm simply saying to have some extra money on hand at home just in case any issues arise.

It is not unknown for banks to close for a period of time in an economic event to allow things to settle down and to also deter what is known as a "bank run"

A bank run occurs when word spreads that the banks are having serious financial problems and literally do not have enough cash on hand to cover their customer's account balances.

This spurs people to panic and dash to the banks to withdraw their money before the banks fail.

Their money is locked up with zero available, or heavily-reduced daily withdrawal limits, until the regulators who insure the deposits have stepped in and produced the cash needed to get things in order.

You may have seen, when you open an account, it will say that the account holder is insured up to a certain amount by the authority responsible for that in your country or region.

For example, in the United States, this would be the FDIC (Federal Deposit Insurance Corporation).

If you wish to understand how this works in comprehensive detail, I suggest you spend some time doing your own research on the matter.

This is insurance on your money if the bank fails.

Not for if it closes for a period of time to get matters in order and deter a bank run.

So, it is possible in an economic event to find yourself unable to access your money for a while.

This does not mean the bank has failed, as I stated above.

They have just restricted your ability to access your money for a period of time.

They will get your money in order for you.

It just may take a little while.

This could be what happens during a transition from the old currencies to the new digital ones

You may be thinking, "Well, if they are going to move to new digital currencies, then why keep any old money outside of the bank?"

Because it will most likely not be an overnight transition.

As I said, earlier, there would be a run-up to transition in that scenario.

If they are going to take the "desirable necessity" path, then it will take time.

If a crash happens and the currencies are not fully ready, then it will definitely take time.

Could be days, weeks, who knows?

But it won't be hours.

Perhaps, it will be a smooth transition without any chaos to trigger the new currency being brought in.

In that case, then no harm done, you simply deposit any paper cash you have into the bank.

But, if it is caused by a scenario as I described above, then you will be glad to have some cash in hand if the banks do close for a short while.

Better to have it and not need it, than need it and not have it…

Think of it in terms of what you would do if you lost all your i.d.

You need to access your money, but it was going to take a few days, or a week or two, to get access to your accounts.

You would need to have some cash on hand to cover food and gas etc.

Think of it like that.

How much money is a good amount?

Honestly, this is down to your own discretion.

If you think you could tide over with a few hundred of your currency, then that is your choice.

If you think it may be wise to have more, then do as you see fit with regards to your personal situation.

Be aware that it is not unheard of for prices on everyday items to surge in price due to scarcity.

If the financial system is in turmoil and banks are implementing various measures, such as closing their doors for a few days, this can knock on to companies and their ability to do business with suppliers.

This can disrupt deliveries, cause delays, and therefore scarcity of products in supermarkets, gas stations etc.

The impact of this can vary from country to country, so do not expect to suddenly find empty shelves overnight.

But also do not count out the possibility that things may not be as easy to come by as they are today and prices may be notably higher until things settle down.

If you do not think that the banks can have problems with covering deposits etc, I suggest you look into what happened in the Repo market in Sept, Oct, Nov, of 2019.

Have a look around on Google and YouTube.

Also, look into how there was a spate of people all over the world not being able to withdraw money and transfers went "missing" for a day or two due to "technical difficulties" across multiple banks across the globe.

The economy was booming and the outbreak was in the following year.

Draw your own conclusions as to how things were really going, even before the outbreak.

I'll leave it at that.

Build up a reserve in the bank.

I'm sure eyebrows are raised at this considering that in the last section I was talking about the potential of banks being closed and needing cash on hand.

No matter what, you are still going to have to pay your bills and almost everyone today is set up via direct debit.

Life will go on in a recession, depression, or full-blown crash scenario.

Whatever scenario is occurring around the transition period.

When you mention severe economic events or even a collapse, people tend to think of some of the more extreme prepper communities who think everything is going to go "Mad Max"

Some people out there will not have you following the practical steps in this book, but will rather advise you to head to the hills and live off the land while fending off marauders looking for food.

I honestly and truly do not believe we will get even close to such a crazy set of circumstances.

I think this is a great way to sell certain goods via fear-mongering, but I do not see it as a reality in our lifetimes.

Who knows for certain what the future holds.

I know I don't, and neither do they.

To be realistic, and to take a practical approach, most economic experts will say it is a good practice to have at least 6 months of living expenses in the bank.

This, in my opinion, is a good idea even in booming economic times.

Few people's incomes are truly safe.

They may have a job one day and find out they are fired, or the company has gone under the very next day.

Happens all the time.

Daily, across the world, I would wager.

A person cannot guarantee they are not going to have an accident that leaves them unable to work or perhaps prevents them from being in the same field due to physical injury.

Again, this happens to people every day.

To think that any of us are immune to this happening is quite frankly ridiculous.

Having a reserve cushion of money in the bank is not only prudent but an imperative in my eyes.

Six months reserve may just save you from being evicted because you can't pay your mortgage or rent because you lost your job or had your hours cut.

As I type this, the moratorium that prevents people from getting evicted is due to end.

I think this alone is going to cause problems.

There are millions of people due to get evicted.

What problems this will cause, besides the social issues, remains to be seen at this point.

But it is not going to be good for the economy.

Many of these people may have been ignoring their rent payments, but still paying their power, cable bills, etc.

Not for much longer.

We shall see how that unfolds and the impact it has.

In my opinion, you should start to build up a cushion as fast as you possibly can.

It doesn't have to be 6 months.

It can be whatever you think is best for you.

If you want a year or just 3 months, then that is your choice.

Too many people today live paycheck to paycheck, and trust me when I say, they will regret it immensely if we do have an event and a recession or depression kicks in.

I feel for the people who can't build a cushion due to their circumstances and I wish them all the best.

My heart goes out to them and I hope fortune helps them through to better times.

The people who could have easily taken basic financial precautions but who decided to blow every penny they earned just to play the social media dress-up game instead.

On their heads be it.

Not my concern.

You may also be thinking,

"Well a few pages ago, you mentioned that the old currencies may become worthless or be converted at a lower ratio into the new digital denomination?"

The fact remains, in or out of the bank, you are going to have to convert that cash at some stage anyway, or it will become greatly devalued while sitting in your bedroom safe.

At least in the bank it is, hopefully, covered by the insurance on that account.

Remember earlier I mentioned the FDIC?

Whatever is in the bank will be converted into the new currencies at whatever rate is set.

Address current debt.

A lot of people are currently paying their bills, and even their rent, on credit cards.

Hopefully, this is a short-term problem for most.

But sooner or later the piper is going to want to be paid.

Everyone's financial situation is different, so this is not a "one size fits all" suggestion.

If you are carrying credit card debt, or any other kind of debt, I would simply look at how long you can maintain payments at this stage.

Don't get me wrong, if you are in a fabulous position and could pay off debt without it affecting your reserves and ability to last financially, then do what you think is best for you.

Having lower monthly expenses, such as credit card bills, is always beneficial.

If, however, like most people, you are not in that position, then I would personally look towards long-term maintenance of payments.

Set aside an amount that matches the total of your payments over several months, minimum.

If you have a monthly debt payment total of, let's say, $300, then look towards keeping perhaps $1800 to one side purely for payment maintenance.

This way, if we do end up on another on lockdown, or if you lose your income, you have at least six months to maneuver without worrying about debt bills not being paid.

I'm not saying any potential situation will last six months.

Neither am I saying it will not last longer, or at least the economic ramifications.

No one knows.

The green shoots optimists.

Those oblivious to reality.

The doom peddlers.

The media

Me.

You.

No one.

We simply do not know how all this is going to pan out and how long it will take to get to a comfortable place again if it does occur.

It could all be a historic footnote rather quickly, or it could be an ongoing concern for a longer period.

Put aside what you decide is a comfortable amount based on your own situation.

When everything does settle down, and it will eventually one way or another, then you can look at the life lessons you learn and apply them in the future.

If you can clear your debt off completely, then consider doing so.

Not at the expense of your reserves or potential investing money, but if it's a viable option to become debt-free, then it's a beneficial move as opposed to keeping it around.

As you will most likely already be aware, there is good debt and bad debt.

Debt for buying assets can be beneficial if managed correctly.

Debt for buying nonsense is always detrimental and should be avoided.

Acquire Essentials.

Well, I'm sure you all witnessed the panic buying and empty shelves in the media or in person.

As it stands at the current point, if you have supplies on hand, then I suggest the following.

Firstly, do not buy two week's worth, consume it all, then go out and buy another two week's worth.

You may get caught out sooner or later and encounter empty shelves.

Many did last time.

Keep a stash of tinned goods and other essentials such as water tucked away and do not touch them.

How much is up to you.

I suggest two week's worth, at least, but do what you think is best for you and your situation.

If you think you can relax with less or desire more.

Do what you think is best.

Aside from this, have a working supply stash that you live on day to day.

A week's worth, two week's worth, whatever you think is best for you.

Too many people were busily munching their way through their panic-induced supply hoard thinking it would either all be over by the time it ran out, or they could simply go out and restock at will.

As it turned out, things got back on track at supermarkets relatively quickly.

But, if there is a major economic event, it may not be the case next time.

Keep your working supply and emergency stash separate.

If things go bad and the shelves empty out again, then you still have a stash to tide you over until you can reload up on supplies.

Also, a note to point out.

During the previous panic buying situation, there were plenty of accounts of people being greedy and selfish.

Arguments, and even fights, broke out as people piled up their carts with items such as water and everyone else be damned.

Look, I'm not saying put yourself and your family second to strangers, but also don't, to be quite blunt, be a scumbag.

If you have multiple cases of water or other items and you see an elderly person or perhaps a family looking at an empty cart and empty shelves.

Give them a case or two from your cart before you head off to pay or continue shopping.

If you have six cases, then handing one or two over to a senior who has none is the right thing to do.

The more we are considerate towards each other, the easier things will be.

Selfish scumbags just make things harder for everyone.

Do not become a scumbag and join in with the selfish mentality.

There are plenty of scumbags as it is, we do not need any more people joining in.

On the other hand, if you do not have items you need and spot someone loaded up with them in their cart, I advise you to leave them as is.

Do not approach them and start trying to reprimand them or demand some of the goods out of fairness.

There were reports of such incidents turning into physical altercations.

Something to remember is that you will run out of patience long before you run out of idiots in today's society.

Don't get into a situation with an idiot because it will always end up in idiotic results.

Some people will get verbally aggressive and others will even get physically aggressive with very little provocation these days.

Often such incidents end up with one person going to the hospital and one person going to jail.

Which one do you prefer as your end result?

Leave the idiots to their idiocy.

Rest assured, life will sort them out eventually.

Idiots produce idiotic results for themselves.

Let life sort them out.

A way around all of this is to shop as early as you possibly can.

This is great for multiple reasons.

Firstly, the shelves have usually been replenished overnight.

Secondly, there are fewer people around and it is usually easier to find parking, etc.

Fewer people equals shorter lines and also fewer idiots.

Also, people tend to be less stressed earlier in the day.

As the day goes on, and the idiots have been in circulation aggravating people, then tension levels tend to rise in general.

I personally find that if I shop before or around 9 am, the people I encounter are scarce, and also more relaxed.

If I shop later in the day, people are stressed due to dealing with crowds, traffic, day-to-day life, and of course, idiots.

No village has reported their idiot missing that I am aware of, so rest assured, there are idiots in circulation in your area.

Avoid them, and shop early while they are usually still rotting in bed.

Reduce Spending.

At this stage of the game, I strongly suggest that everyone monitors their spending.

If you usually fritter money on things you do not need, then I suggest you slow down.

A way to curb this, and to also preserve your cash reserves, is to not buy things such as chocolate, soda, alcohol, etc.

Firstly, such things are needless and bad for you anyway for the most part.

If you are sitting at home night after night in front of the T.V and drinking beers while munching chips and chocolate.

Expect to gain needless pounds.

Secondly, let's say you get through $10 worth of such things a day.

Chocolate bar here and a beer there.

That's $300 a month.

If you are doing such things and care to work out how much it is costing you, then you may find that $10 is on the low end.

In this current economic situation, or any kind of downturn in the future, everyone needs to watch their spending.

If you lose your income at some point, then every penny is going to count.

Your bills will come in, rain or shine, I assure you of that.

What's the wisest policy?

Putting money to one side or drinking and munching it away?

That $300 may cover some bills in the future.

There are so many things I could put on this list besides chocolate etc.

It could be that you smoke or buy new video games as soon as they release.

All manner of things.

Take a look at your spending and see what can be eliminated.

Every penny you have in reserve is a part of your future financial security.

I'm not saying live like a hermit or don't enjoy life.

I'm saying that every penny you waste is a penny you don't have in reserve for emergencies and a penny you are not using to make money, either from the current mania or a future economic scenario.

Sell Off Unwanted Items.

It is easier than ever to sell things online.

A lot, if not most, people shop online on a regular basis.

The trend now is that many people actually prefer it to shopping at traditional stores.

I know I do.

Less hassle, usually cheaper, and often a better selection.

If you have unwanted items at home, you can always consider posting them online, perhaps eBay for example.

I personally have not used eBay for many years, but they still have plenty of traffic last I heard.

There are plenty of reputable places to sell online if you care to search.

Consider going through your home and getting rid of some things you don't want.

They may end up selling and bringing in some money you can put into your reserves or towards your investments.

If you have things laying around that you no longer use, and may have value, then why not.

Do not sell things for the sake of it, but if it's a choice between paying your bills and perhaps investing, or keeping those golf clubs you used twice seven years ago...

You get my point.

As you are clearing through your excess belongings, you will find things that you may not be able to sell.

Simply donate these things to your local charity.

It is never a bad thing to help others and it is something that we all should endeavor to do when possible.

With the potential coming financial turmoil, there are going to be a lot of people who are going to need help.

Even as I write this, the homeless problem is becoming a serious issue and it will, in my opinion, be multiple times worse when the economic situation impacts across the board.

So rather than just discard some old blankets or leave them in a closet taking up space needlessly, donate them to a homeless charity.

We tend to forget that not all homeless people are there due to situations of their own making via poor life choices etc.

Some people simply had a bad run of luck and didn't have anyone to turn to.

Families are typically a lot smaller than they used to be.

In the past, it was not uncommon for families to be composed of five or more siblings.

Today, being an only child is actually more common than being one of three siblings.

If a person falls on hard times and their family has passed away, then they simply may not have anyone to lean on in times of hardship.

As I said, bear in mind, that I personally think that we are going to see a lot of people every day people who have not put themselves in that position due to their own poor decisions, but find themselves out of work, out of money, and out of luck.

Have some compassion and do what you can to help.

Those blankets that mean nothing to you may mean a great deal to someone else.

You may be thinking, "hold on, this book started about economic crashes and digital currencies, and now we are talking about giving blankets to the homeless and selling stuff on eBay!"

Hears the logic.

Firstly, help people out if you can.

Why not?

Secondly, money you have sitting in nonsense you don't want or need can be used to profit from what may be coming,

R.A.D (Reserves, Assets, Debt)

A system I personally use is what I term as R.A.D.

Reserves, Assets, Debt.

I have not reinvented the wheel here so do not expect a secret sauce for financial success.

I do however find it has, does, and expect it to continue, to work for me.

It is a very simple concept.

Any spare income you may have past your bills and living expenses is divided into 3 and split amongst the categories.

For example, if you have $600 a month spare after your bills and living money, then put $200 into each category.

First of all, let me describe what each category is.

Reserves is exactly what it says on the tin.

Reserve money.

This may be your savings account, cash on hand, whatever setup you may have.

Assets are stocks, bullion, crypto, business start-up money etc.

Debt is credit cards and any other debt you may be trying to eliminate from your life.

You can of course assign anything you want to these categories.

If you just wish to get some extra cash in the bank, pay down a credit card, and buy a few stocks, then that is your R.A.D. framework.

It really is up to you how you handle this.

I merely present the concept as a simple way to see progression in all aspects of your financial life simultaneously.

Sometimes people will advise you to just plough everything into clearing your debt off before worrying about buying assets etc.

Get back to zero debt before trying to build up kind of mentality.

With this system, I find that it actually inspires people to work harder at improving their financial situation.

If someone is working themselves to the bone to clear debt alone, then it can be very demotivating and disheartening to be constantly giving the fruits of your labor away and have nothing to show for it except a balance remaining each month.

Granted, battling compounding interest is not to be dismissed.

But neither is seeing your reserves and asset base increase at the same time your debt balance is decreasing.

It is a very simple concept that anyone can implement regardless of the amount you are able, and choose, to commit each time you have money come in.

If you are reading this and thinking "I don't have any spare money each month" then do not forget what I said about reducing your spending in the earlier part of this book.

Also, continue reading to see what I have to say about creating more income as we go along through the book.

Give the concept some thought and see if it is something you may, or may not, choose to implement based on your financial situation and plans.

You should be looking to constantly add to your reserves in this very uncertain time.

A lot of people may end up being laid off or at least have their hours cut as some companies reposition themselves if we enter a future event as I have mentioned.

Learn about the stock market and set up a trading account.

The global markets reacted to the outbreak with a roller coaster ride for investors, to say the least.

The Dow dropped from the 29k range in the later part of February 2020 and sank as low as the 18k range during March.

There was a lot of economic uncertainty caused by the announcement of the outbreak and markets reacted in a spectacular fashion.

The outbreak news, combined with the lockdowns effect on most businesses, spooked the markets.

Perhaps in the scenario of another major future lockdown things may look different.

Could be better or worse.

We shall see.

If you are a trader or thinking of getting into the stock market, then I would consider the following.

A lot of businesses are recovering at the moment, but, as I said earlier, we could see another lockdown later in the year.

Japan is currently tightening up as other regions are easing back restrictions.

Even in the regions that are starting to open back up towards normality, things are still not back to how they were.

A lot of people are either tightening their spending, blowing through their money, or have reduced or no income.

This is global.

Even now the lockdowns are pretty much lifted, there is still a lot of economic fallout.

I think the shrewd have not dashed out spending at the first hint of normality and I don't think a lot of other people have been able to.

This will start showing up in quarterly reports for businesses.

I do not expect any upcoming quarters in the short term to get off to a good start.

Economists typically class two consecutive quarters in which GDP declines as a recession.

I'll be highly shocked if we do not meet that criteria in due course.

Assuming we do not have a full-blown global economic crash in the meantime.

The U.S. is typically considered a global temperature gauge in my opinion.

If the U.S. is not doing well, then other less robust economies are usually not faring well.

Also, the U.S. is a very large part of global consumption.

A lot of countries rely on American trade as a significant part of their own GDP.

There are many strong economies in the world besides the U.S. but the U.S. is the largest in the world by multiple trillions of dollars.

California alone has a GDP larger than most nations on earth.

The U.S. will always bounce back over time, as will most nations.

But the current situation going forward is not looking too shiny.

If you are reading this book during the apparent tail end of this current outbreak, then I would keep a close eye on the U.S. markets and economic situation.

If it is in the future and you are experiencing another economic event, then I would still look to the U.S. if they are still the number one economy.

Due to the lockdowns across the globe, many industries such as airlines, hotels, casinos, cruise lines, and luxury got slammed.

Will they recover in the future?

As industries, I suspect so.

As individual companies?

Time will tell.

Select some stocks you may be interested in and research how they have reacted to this current situation.

Compare their prices before, during, and currently.

See what caused them to fall and rise.

Read into their industries and see how they typically react in past crisis situations and recovery, then work out how you think they will react if we go into another lockdown.

This will set you up ready for any future scenarios.

Here are some terms for you to be aware of.

In the investing world, there are terms such as,

"Do not catch a falling knife" and "Dead cat bounce"

The first means, when a stock stabilizes after a major fall and investors call a bottom too early, then buy up the stock expecting it to start rising.

Shortly after, the stock resumes its drop in price and the investors lose money.

They get "cut" because they tried to catch the stock while it was still falling.

Think of the people who bought into Bitcoin as it fell from $60k on its way to the low $30k range it eventually settled at.

Rest assured there were people who bought in at $50k, $45k, etc.

This is "Catching a falling knife"

A "Dead cat bounce" is when a stock drops significantly, stabilizes, then starts going back up in value before resuming its decline in price.

Past the point it stabilized at before.

Investors can get caught up in this very easily, either through greed, lack of information, or pure bad luck.

Why do I bring these terms up?

If you are going to start investing, or continue if you are already involved, then you need to learn some of the logic.

You will hear terms such as "Buy the dip"

It has been thrown around a lot on social media whenever Bitcoin takes a downturn.

"It's just a dip. Buy the dip. Bitcoins going to the moon!"

You may have seen that kind of thing on social media yourself.

Now think back to what I just wrote about "Catching a falling knife" and "Dead cat bounce"

Many people saw the dip in Bitcoin back in early 2018 after it soared to $20k in late 2017.

The cries of "Buy the dip" were plentiful.

Some people did.

$18k

$16k

$12k

They "caught a falling knife" as it made its way down to $6k.

Now, this is not to say they haven't held on and are now sitting on coins they bought for $15k that are now worth $38k or even sold out at $60k a couple of weeks ago.

But, do you think they felt great back in early 2018?

Do you think they could have made other money with their capital over the last 3 years they spent waiting for Bitcoin to start its current surge?

I'm just using it as an example of the "Catching a falling knife" concept.

At the current time, crypto trading is like a modern-day gold rush.

If you can make money from it, then all the more power to you.

Make hay while the sun shines.

But just be aware of the points I have made and make up your own mind on them.

If I'm wrong, then no harm done.

If I'm right, then you do not want to have your fortunes tied up in crypto coins that have been frozen or are not allowed to be converted into the new digital currencies because they will cause inflation.

Learn stocks, and you will see why shortly.

Be aware of the situation.

Be sure to keep an eye on what is going on in the world, and also in your own, country, city, and area.

The mainstream media will tell you this and that, but they are either usually late, hold things back, or tone them down in my experience.

Just because the media shows that one place is doing well and everyone is out shopping, it does not mean that is the overall truth for the world or your country or area.

Even now, the mainstream is pushing the general idea that things are getting back to normal and things are looking to start booming again.

Yes, the markets are up from their dramatic drops, but based on what?

Lots of businesses closed due to the lockdowns and plenty are in serious financial trouble still.

A lot of people are running out of money and seem to think there will be plenty more rounds of stimulus going forward.

I suspect that a lot of people are going to get laid off when the next lockdown takes effect.

As I type this, a lot of places had a surge of spending from the recent round of stimulus checks a few weeks back.

That is all well and good, but most of that money has been spent already.

Now what?

Are things going to roll along without any more rounds?

If you are not in the U.S., how are people and businesses faring in your area?

Make your own decisions and maneuvers based on your own research and intelligence.

Do not allow the media to spoon-feed you "facts" and blindly follow what they say.

Sometimes they are right, and sometimes they are not.

Gamble as you will.

It's your choice.

No one knows for certain how things are going to go.

I know I don't.

Neither do they.

As I have stated many times throughout this book.

Before you invest a penny in anything or make any kind of financial moves, you should ensure that you do your own research and possibly consult professionals.

There are many people who post all kinds of opinions online and spout off on TV about financial matters during the best of times, let alone during a crisis.

A lot of people got HEAVILY burned financially by listening to so-called "experts" on TV and online during the 08 crash.

People saying "Everything was OK" and "Not to worry, things are stabilizing and starting to trend upwards"

People who claimed they knew how things were going to go and telling people where to invest and what to do as the best course of action.

People got SLAMMED listening to them.

Please do your own research before attempting any financial moves or investments.

Anyone can put a shirt and tie on and speak with confidence.

But no one knows for sure how any financial crisis will unfold.

One thing you should start to do from this very moment is to take time every day to stay aware of the current situation.

I'm not going to list any specific websites or video channels, but they are easy to find with simple searches.

Terms related to your desired topic will set you off on your path to finding information online.

Be warned you will find some nonsense and doom-mongers along the way.

Fear sells as they say.

But there are plenty of reliable and genuine sites and channels that will keep you on top of current matters.

In fact, there are some that will inform you of things way before the news hits the mainstream channels and sites.

Typically, the mainstream is not going to mention anything until after the fact if history is to repeat itself.

I'll put it this way.

There were rumblings of this outbreak circulating online back in January of 2020.

Some quite detailed information.

The mainstream denounced it all as nonsense and conspiracy theory.

But, come late March and early April, the media were touting most, if not all, of the same information as "breaking" and claiming they were at the cutting edge of keeping the public informed.

Find sources you believe to be genuine, are usually accurate in a timely manner, and stay current with what they have to say.

As I said earlier, keep your eyes open.

If not, you only have yourself to blame if you find yourself in the huge heap of people who will also fall down the financial stairs.

It's up to you what you want to implement or discard.

My aim is simply to get you thinking and hopefully acting in your own favor.

It's up to you what you want to implement or discard.

Look for opportunities.

All of the examples coming up next are exactly that.

Examples.

I mention them as an illustration of the concept of profiting from a financial situation.

There are many opportunities to be found in all economic cycles.

Booms, busts, and recoveries.

Do not see a financial event as the end of the world, look for silver linings in the clouds as they say.

Do not bite off more than you can chew, but do not miss out on your potential slice of the pie either.

People will be crushed in future economic cycles and others will make fortunes.

But it all depends on a variety of factors and a firm base in research and professional consultation.

Some people are currently looking for opportunities by riding the volatility in the stock market.

Others are speculating in crypto coins.

Some are starting online businesses to capitalize on the trend towards online shopping, but also as a hedge against future lockdown scenarios.

As I said earlier, I think we are close to another lockdown.

While traditional stores were closed, online stores boomed.

Even YouTubers and other content creators saw a rise in earnings as people were stuck indoors all day with nothing to do except trawl around online.

Before we move into the actual wealth aspects of this book, we need to get something in line.

You need to optimize your mindset.

You can be as prepared as possible and can have all kinds of knowledge and information.

But you will not reach your true potential without the correct mindset.

Mindset - Existence vs Empire.

With the potential opportunities coming our way, you need to have the correct mindset.

What are you trying to achieve overall?

I mean the really big picture.

The end goal.

Are you investing just to be able to buy expensive items so you can "flex" or are you thinking more long-term?

For me, personally, I view it like this.

Are you trying to build an Existence or an Empire?

In order to build an existence, all you need to do is work out what kind of lifestyle you want, and how much per month/year you are going to need to achieve and maintain.

It is that simple at its core.

If you just want to replace your job income to ensure financial security and that is all you care about.

Simply look at what you want to earn, what kind of life you want to live, and how to achieve the required income.

If you earn five thousand per month but want to get out of your job and live a ten thousand a month lifestyle till you die, then you have planned an existence.

You can set up a business that produces what you need, maintain it, and you are set.

Or you can invest and chase gains as fast as you can get them.

And probably spend them just as fast.

However, if you say, ok, I want to be a millionaire via real estate, produce twenty thousand dollars a month in residual income via rent, and leave the assets to my children.

Well, you are looking at building an empire.

Significantly different processes and mindset are needed.

Building an existence is actually a short-term mindset.

You are looking purely to have the desired amount of money each month.

The process is designed around this and you will aim to achieve this as fast as you possibly can.

Building an empire is a long-term mindset.

You are thinking in processes that can take, and last, years and decades.

If you have a business, then sure you can pass it on to your kids when you want to.

Teach them the process, and off they go chasing monthly income.

If you leave them a portfolio of well-managed real estate that produces income year in year out on autopilot.

Well, your kids have the income and are also free to go off to do their own thing, including setting up a business.

Do you see the difference?

As I said, similar, but significantly different as far as mindset and process to setup.

I'm not going to go deep into what differences there are between setting up a business and a real estate empire.

I would assume that's more than apparent.

My point is the mindset.

An existence mindset is designed to provide for you "now" so long as you work at it.

An empire mindset is designed to provide for you long-term and pretty much run itself.

A huge business, can, of course, become an empire.

Look at Microsoft, Apple, Amazon, etc.

The owners are famous and employ hundreds of thousands of people.

But do you think that the founders kept a short-term income mindset when building those companies?

So long as they could maintain their lifestyle with a good monthly income, then all is good?

No, of course not.

They all went in with the long-term empire mindset.

Their process involved acquisitions, expansions, and allocation of revenue into enlarging the company in a steady growth trajectory.

It's not running on the concept of,

"So long as I have enough to pay my bills and do what I want, then I'm content."

Massive difference in mindset, approach, process, and of course, results,

Now, this is not to say, you should aim to build a huge empire that is going to take you most of your life.

My advice, that I practice personally is this.

Your mindset will be dictated by your goals.

If you are just aiming to clear debt and quit your job, then you should be in a small time-frame mindset.

You are aiming for small numbers and therefore it shouldn't take decades to achieve.

However, if you are serious that you want to be a multi-millionaire and leave a huge legacy for your kids.

Well, you, sooner or later, will have to change your mindset from short-term existence to long-term empire.

The core factors are the same.

You will still need focus, self-discipline, time allocation skills, a desire, etc.

But, your processes will be different.

In an existence mindset, money is a form of short-term gratification.

So long as you earn the required amount to live your life, you are successful at your goals.

In an empire mindset, you are looking to earn money in order to retain and expand your asset base.

Simply put, existence mindset puts disposable income over assets and eliminates debt.

Empire mindset puts assets over disposable income and utilizes debt in order to expand its asset base.

Whole different game.

In an existence mindset, revenue is desired in order to create a lifestyle.

In an empire mindset, revenue is desired in order to expand the empire.

Hopefully, that may be a little bit clearer on what I am trying to convey.

A typical existence-minded person will either live comfortably and treat themselves, with few, if any, asset-building plans.

Or they will blow the money left and right to enjoy their desired lifestyle.

Cars, mansions, watches, clothes, vacations.

Empire-minded people typically do not worry about those things, only assets and expansion.

In an existence mindset, the individual is the priority and center stage.

In an empire mindset, the empire is priority and center stage.

Look at some of the richest empire people in the world and how they live.

Warren Buffet lives in a modest home, drives a regular car, and dresses conservatively.

Steve Jobs was known for his black top and jeans outfit.

Warren Buffet, even in his younger days, was not bothered about sports cars and huge mansions.

He was bothered about building Berkshire Hathaway, his empire.

That is where all his time, focus, and revenue went.

Look at your average celebrity these days.

Their whole mindset is they want a great existence.

Cars, mansions, jewelry, clothes.

I'm not saying they do not invest.

I'm saying their mindset is different.

The short-term existence mindset will blow money on clothes that will be out of style in a matter of months or other flashy status trinkets.

The money comes in, and the money goes out.

So long as it keeps coming, the lifestyle is maintained.

The long-term empire mindset will put as much as possible into acquiring assets that produce more revenue.

So even if there is a slowdown in income at some point, they still have revenue coming in from assets that they can sell if they need to.

The money comes in and stays in the form of assets.

Whole different mindset and final results.

If the short-term mindset person loses their income for some reason, their existence level usually goes with it.

If a long-term empire mindset loses their income from one source, they typically have income from other sources and a large net-worth backing them.

I would sooner have a portfolio of boring, but valuable, revenue-producing assets for life, than a garage full of sports cars, and a closet full of designer clothes.

Take time to consider what you are aiming to do for yourself.

I'm not talking about building a six-month reserve and clearing your debt.

I'm talking long-term.

Are you aiming to just replace your job income in order to have financial security and then leave it at that?

An Existence mindset.

Or are you aiming to replace your job income and then focus on building more income streams and an assets portfolio?

An Empire mindset.

If it appears that you are in an existence-type mindset, then ask yourself.

Are you happy with that?

If you are, then great.

Finish this book and get to work on your goals!

If you are in that mindset, but not happy about it, then what should you do?

The answer is actually quite simple.

Change your goals to reflect the difference.

If you have lots of short-term goals that may not be that important, then eliminate them and replace them.

For example, if you have been thinking of treating yourself to an expensive watch once you have achieved your financial independence, then simply spend the money on dividend stocks or setting up a business instead.

It really can be that simple at this stage.

There are many kinds of assets you can buy, not just stocks, crypto, or setting up a business.

Do your research and see what appeals to you and then, as always, get professional advice.

However, I will present a few examples here to give you the theme of the concept I'm referring to.

Existence Mindset Goals and Acquisitions.

Luxury Watch.

Vacation.

Mansion.

Sports Car.

Small business or investment income to fund it all.

Empire Mindset Goals and Acquisitions.

Dividend Stocks.

Rental Properties.

Bonds.

Multiple Residual Income Streams, such as books, digital products.

A large business such as a corporation that owns multiple small businesses.

Although far from complete or comprehensive, the above list displays what I am referring to.

If I were to put a phrase to describe the concept it would be this.

Existence mindset consists of you working for money.

Empire mindset consists of making money work for you

As I said earlier, the other big difference is the time frames involved.

Existence mindset is all about now and instant gratification.

Empire mindset is all about long-term thinking and delayed gratification.

Truth be told, existence mindset is what most people function on..

In my opinion, existence mindset is dangerously close to the bad habits that hold most people back in the first place.

After all, if you spend recklessly with a normal income, increasing your income and freedom will simply give you more scope and freedom to behave the same way on a bigger scale.

If your goal list consists of luxury watches, etc, then perhaps this is something you should address before you even start.

This is not to say you shouldn't have rewards involved in your progression system.

However, the mainstay of your goals should be directed towards the acquisition of assets for your empire, not the acquisition of status items.

There is nothing wrong with saying, "OK, if I clear my debt and build up $20k of dividends, then I can treat myself"

This falls into the incentive and motivation.

Setting a reward for yourself if you achieve a certain goal and using that to spur yourself on.

As you advance along with your plans and experience the process it takes to acquire money.

You will most likely start to want to hold on to your hard-earned money anyway.

I'm sure you have heard people talk about how the rich are greedy, and some are very tight with their money.

Do you know why that is?

They understand money.

Usually, the people making derogatory claims about the rich hoarding money don't have much money themselves because they do not understand it.

The rich understand that money can be easy to acquire, but also realize it can be wasted at a far greater speed than it comes if placed in the wrong hands.

They also understand that your money should work for you, not vice versa.

You will also hear people say that:

"Money can't buy you happiness."

"Money is not that important to me."

"Money is the root of all evil."

Let me clarify something.

Money can't buy you happiness, but it is needed for almost everything else required in life.

Try going to pay your bills with only a gleeful smile and no money.

Attempt to convince your bank or landlord, that your mortgage or rent doesn't need paying in money, just goodwill to all people.

Do you get my point?

Remember, money is an exchange for goods or services in most cases.

Goods and services take time and effort to provide.

A price is what is required to recover the initial expenditure of resources such as material and labor, with a profit incentive added.

Money is important, not as important as health or family, but it ranks up there.

That's immune to debate in my opinion.

You have to eat, be clothed, and have a place to live.

Unless you join some kind of wild cult or commune, trust me, you are going to need money.

Today, tomorrow, and for the rest of your life.

Do not ever let some fool convince you even slightly that money isn't important.

If someone does, tell them you will gladly, and with a smile, take any money of theirs they don't want.

Watch their reaction; you won't get a penny off them.

As I have said throughout this book, there are a lot of people experiencing financial hardship.

There are also a lot of people buying up every asset in sight.

It will be magnified many times over on both sides if the financial transition to digital occurs through economic chaos as I think it will.

When everything settles, which it will at some point, some people will be ruined, others will be back to where they were before, and others will be richer than ever.

Which do you have in mind for yourself?

Run Your Life Like A Business.

Around ten or so years ago, I went to a tax professional with my ex-wife.

It was tax time, we had to file, and I like to have it done professionally as opposed to guessing my way through trying to file myself.

Anyhow, the guy we spoke to was, I would say, in his late twenties, or thereabout.

I was in my early thirties at that time.

I was money-hungry but didn't know a fraction of what I know now.

I still have a lot to learn today and will continue learning till the day I keel over for good.

Everyone has room to grow and learn, and that will never change.

We were sitting with a pile of folders and going through the motions.

I was getting bored to be honest because we had already sat out in the lobby for the best part of an hour waiting due to an appointment backlog.

In any case, this young gentleman introduced me to a concept that changed the way I thought about my life forever.

He was looking over our paperwork and said:

"Ok, I want you to learn how to run your life like a business."

He went on to detail how we should do this, and I listened eagerly.

After all was said and done, if the truth be known, a lot of what he had said was neither here nor there to me.

However, that one statement sat with me.

Me, being me, I went on to research, adapt, and modify this concept to my own liking.

May I pause for a moment and suggest you should take that attitude with all the concepts I introduce you to.

In this book, I am not trying to give you set in stone unbending blueprints.

You should take what I tell you and adopt, modify, and discard as you see fit.

This book aims to change the way you think and approach aspects of your life.

Some things you may agree with and find useful.

Others just simply may not resonate with you.

Nothing wrong with that.

In truth, I like the fact that you may be able to improve on my concepts.

I also like that you are paying attention enough to be able to come to the conclusion that a concept is not for you.

This means the book, and me, are doing what was intended.

You are thinking about how to improve your life and actively moving towards success post-crash.

That alone there is worth the time taken to read my ideas.

Now, how do I now view this concept of "Run your life like a business?"

A business has several traits in regard to this.

Businesses have an operating expense account.

Running costs, such as bills and payroll expenses, are projected ahead of time and are always being assessed for ways to reduce them in favor of profit margins.

Goals for the year and business quarters are planned and aggressively aimed for.

There are always plans and efforts directed towards future expansion.

After all is said and done, the core objective of the business is revenue.

So, how does this translate into my concept?

Businesses have an operating expense account and project expenses ahead of time.

A business, especially a new one, needs to have cash on hand to pay for the general day to day running costs.

These can be things like payroll, stationery, marketing, whatever the business needs simply to function.

I now operate on a similar framework for my day-to-day life.

I have sat down and gone through my bills and typical essential spending such as food, gas, etc.

This has provided me with a number that is pretty stable and reflects my typical monthly spending.

I now have a pretty damn accurate set of numbers I need to have in that account for things to run without hick-up for a month, a quarter, and a year.

My reserves also are structured around being able to survive without income for set periods of time and cover any unexpected expenses.

Now I know these numbers, I know how to use my R.A.D. allocations to optimum effect.

When money comes in, I know exactly how much must go into my operating expense account before I can start allocating for Reserves, Assets, and Debt.

Using this system of an operating expense account and the R.A.D combined has truly changed my life for the better.

It has simplified my finances as far as outgoings.

I no longer have to worry about x amount of individual bills because it is just one number I have to think about.

The monthly operating expense number.

This drastically declutters your mind and reduces stress.

It also allows me to invest with a greater degree of certainty of what amount I can afford.

Here is an example of how simple it can be.

George sits and works out his monthly expenses.

After all is totaled, George comes to the conclusion that all his bills combined come to $2783 a month.

He also notices that sometimes his power bills fluctuate due to seasonal changes and that some other bills move up or down a few dollars a month.

He decides to round that number off to $3000 to account for fluctuations.

After looking at his typical spending and general living expenses such as haircuts, food, going out, clothes, etc.

A rough average of around $1800 a month seems to be correct.

George decides to call it $2000.

Income-wise, George averages around $8k a month after taxes.

So, he ensures that he always allocates $5k a month ($3k bills + $2k spending) into his expenses account.

This leaves him with $3k a month left from his $8k income.

George uses the R.A.D system, so he puts $1k into his Reserves account, $1k into his Assets account, and puts $1k towards paying down Debt.

Now George is not stressing himself out thinking about nine different bills, or what he is safe to spend if he wants to buy something as a treat.

He is also building up his Reserves, Assets, and reducing his Debt all at the same time.

George is far less stressed, and he is also very aware of where he is financially.

As you can see, the system is not a bad one!

Simple to set up and maintain.

I honestly think that if more people did this kind of thing, you may just see an overall improvement in the state of people's finances.

You would probably find that people would also be less stressed in general.

The problem is that people tend to neglect to organize their finances and are in a constant state of uncertainty.

Most will blame low income, unexpected expenses, or whatever other excuse they believe justifies the mess around them.

The truth is, with a little bit of organization, they could go a long way to fixing their situation and reducing their stress.

Businesses have plans for the year, business quarters, and future expansion.

You have almost certainly heard the term "Business plan".

A business without a plan is like a ship without a rudder.

Directionless.

Like the ship, it will just drift around or go whichever way the wind blows it.

The vast majority of people go through life like this.

They just drift along and let the tides and storms of life take them where they may.

The original lockdown and the amount of people who suddenly couldn't pay their bills after two weeks attests to this,

If you do not know what your bills are and do not have any financial direction in life, then how do you expect to get anywhere?

With some simple planning and personal financial accounting, you know where you are and where you are going.

My advice to you is to make sure you complete the exercises discussed earlier in this book to take stock of your financial situation.

Then, like a business, project forward your expenses and also your plans for expansion.

You may decide that your next goal is to get six months money in reserve and then implement R.A.D.

To achieve this, you may plan to spend the next few months setting up an online business venture such as a social media account promoting products.

It can be whatever you want it to be.

Have a plan and stay aware of the situation around you, financial and otherwise.

Because rest assured, when this crash takes hold, you are going to be very glad you did.

Aim To Be Financially Independent ASAP

As I have said many times throughout this book, I can see a lot of companies laying off more people during and after the next lockdown.

There is far too much economic hardship and fallout from this outbreak already.

Not many people, or at least not enough, are going to be out spending money left and right when the next one hits, or even after it is lifted.

I hate to say this, and I hope I'm wrong, but I think a lot more people are going to get laid off in the coming months.

Hopefully, I'm wrong, but it's not looking that way.

Is it?

If you can create even a small amount of extra monthly revenue, it may help immensely if you lose your job.

Your main aim should be to replace your income altogether if possible.

Obviously, the best outcome is to build your own income and have enough to invest in R.A.D.

Offline ventures are going to evolve in ways that remain to be seen.

Social distancing and the threat of further future lockdowns for years to come are going to be influential in quite a major way.

Online, in my opinion, is the way to go.

You will see that many businesses will be moving online as the future unfolds.

As I write this, many online shopping platforms reported a sales boom in 2020 as the world was gripped by the pandemic.

Many offline business were crushed by lockdowns and other policies.

If you wish to build an income that is resilient in today's world, online is the way to go in my opinion.

How To Potentially Profit From The Crash

This section is not intended to be a financial blueprint or professional financial advice.

It should not be considered or regarded as such.

It is merely suggestions used to illustrate the mindset concept I am describing.

Before investing a penny into any financial venture you should ensure to do your own research and to consult financial professionals.

Before we move into this next section I want to point out one or two things for those readers that may not be versed in stocks.

You may know stock trading as buying a stock at one price and then selling it later at another, hopefully, higher price.

But did you also know that some stocks pay you money while you own the stock?

These are known as dividend payments.

To keep it simple, some companies pay out a large portion of their profits to shareholders either yearly, quarterly, or even sometimes monthly.

Quarterly is the most common payment schedule because it ties in with quarterly earnings statements etc.

So, to give you an example.

You may buy stock A for $10 a unit.

Stock A pays $1 per year dividend. ($1 divided by 4 quarters = 25 cents every quarter)

So, every 3 months the stock will pay 25 cents to shareholders per stock they own.

If someone purchased $10k worth of stock A (1000 stocks at $10 each) and held on to it, then every quarterly pay date they own the stock, they would be paid 1000 x 25 cents = $250.

Typically dividends remain reasonably consistent over time.

So, even if stock A went to $15 in price, it would still be earning the holder $250 every 3 months, plus their initial holdings would have increased in value from $10k to $15k.

On the other hand, if the stock dropped from $10 down to $7, the holder would still be getting the $250 dividend every 3 months, but would have lost $3k on their initial $10k investment.

But, bear in mind, they have only lost the $3k if they sell the stock at $7.

If they hold it they will still be getting the $250 payment, and also the stock may return to $10 or even go higher over time.

One thing to be cautious of is that if a companies stock price tanks, it may be because the company is in trouble.

If they are in trouble, they may raise the dividend to try and attract new investors, they may reduce it to try and get back on their feet, or they may suspend it for a period of time.

But, give this some consideration.

Let's say that the market crashes and Stock A tanks from $10 down to $4 as investors sell off to get out of the market and to minimize losses.

If you are sitting on the sidelines, with enough spare cash sitting in your trading account, you could buy in and scoop up these $4 dividend stocks.

Now, if it is a crash scenario, then the dividend may be frozen for a period of time, and of course, you need to make sure the company is going to survive and recover.

But, all markets go in cycles, as I said earlier.

If you see a boom, rest assured a bust is coming down the pipe at some stage.

Usually, the bigger the boom, the bigger the bust.

This is why I say the current record stock market highs etc are not as great a sign as people think, and all these new shoeshine investors are convinced the only way is up.

Again, I say, look into 1929.

I don't mean to sound bad about all these new investors by the way.

I think it is fantastic that people are getting involved in their own investing and making great money.

I truly wish them all the best of luck.

My issue is that a portion of them are very vocal and shout as loud as they can that this asset or that coin is going to go up and up.

They are positioning themselves as experts.

That anyone who does not listen to them is an idiot.

The problem is, because they are so vocal, I think they are going to lead a lot of people straight off the financial cliff with them at some point.

Recent China crypto ban debacle, for example?

Granted, you can say,

"Well, why should I listen to you? You have already said you don't consider yourself as, or want to be considered as, an expert or a financial whizz."

Simply because I have been trading for many years and have been keeping a suspicious eye on Bitcoin and other cryptos since somewhere in the region of 2011.

I also am not telling you "This is going to happen, you should invest in this"

I'm giving you my opinion and encouraging you to research for yourself.

A lot of these people have literally been active 12 months, some less, and have only ever dealt with Bitcoin or stocks that they bought on the back of trending hashtags.

A lot of these people would be seriously lost if you sat them in front of a trading screen without social media,

I would like to see some of these people sat in front of a computer with only access to news sites, such as the BBC, etc, and being asked,

"You have access to all current and past articles. Give us your opinion on where oil prices are going and why?"

You could even do the same thing with crypto and they would be lost without access to hashtags.

Again, I think it's great that people are getting involved in trading, both crypto and stocks.

I just think it's a shame, and not a great sign at all, that many of them rely on hashtags to make their trading moves.

Because, as I said, it wouldn't be the first time the #tothemoon crowd has lead a lot of people into a bad loss.

If the things I have talked about do come to pass, and we have a black swan economic event or another lockdown that tips the economy into freefall, a lot of these "experts" will lead people into financial ruin, with their "buy the dip" and #tothemoon warcries.

In this next section, I'm going to list what I think are some sectors you should look at now and in the coming future.

If you learn these things now, and we do have an economic event similar to the one I described, because somethings coming, this mania can't continue, then you could make some serious money.

Generational wealth level money.

While most people are panicking and wondering what is happening, you could be buying up very valuable stocks and assets at cut-rate prices…

If timed correctly, you may also be able to get your old currency parked into stocks that will go back up in value rather than just convert your currency into the new digital at whatever lower rate they offer.

The potential to make a lot of money is there, and also, if you do sell in the future, it will be cashed out in the new digital currency.

No need to worry about any regulations being put in that ban financial institutions from handling your money...

This is not to say dump crypto now and go into stocks.

I'm just saying that if you study now how various assets react in various scenarios, you can make educated decisions on what to do if you see a crash coming.

It is well known that the largest amounts of money are lost and made during a crash.

The average person loses so much money and sells at low prices as panic sets in.

The educated investor waits for such opportunities, and buys the hell out of assets they know will return to value when everything settles down.

Manias make many people rich and panics make some people very wealthy...

One thing you should consider aiming for is to build up a strong portfolio of dividend stocks.

The logic is extremely simple.

If you can build up a solid dividend income, you will have an income coming in no matter what happens in your day-to-day life.

If you build it up high enough, you can replace your job income.

You build it up to whatever level you like.

Some stocks pay monthly dividends and others pay quarterly (Every 3 months)

You may be thinking, "Yeah, but it's going to take a lot of money to build up"

But here's the key.

Keep buying the dividend stocks while they are cheap during the crash.

Make sure the companies are likely to recover.

Pick companies that you know are basically too big to fail.

I can't and won't name individual companies, simply because I am not touting specific stocks.

But, use your brain and you will know which companies will survive and likely flourish when things settle down.

There are some huge well-known companies that pay dividends and they are highly unlikely to go out of business no matter how severe the crash.

They may cut or even suspend their dividend for a while, but it will most likely return at some point.

In fact, if they cut or suspend the dividend payment, the stock will be trading at even lower prices usually.

This means you can pick them up for even cheaper during the crash.

I explained this earlier in this section, so I won't cover it in detail again, but, if you build up as many dividend stocks as you can, you will have aready made income waiting for you when things settle back to normality.

Plus, the stock price will most likely increase in notable amounts.

If the company is still paying the dividend during the aftermath of the crash, even better.

When you get the dividend payment, reinvest it into buying even more of the dividend stock while it is cheap.

Use your dividend income to build your dividend income.

So, although you may be thinking "I need to buy x amount of stock in order to make this much dividend, it's a lot"

Re-investing the dividend will get you there a lot quicker.

Later in the book, I will tell you how to make your own online income.

If you combine this with spending discipline, R.A.D., and dividends…

Be very sure to do your own research and perhaps consult a professional to enable you to make an informed decision before committing any money to a stock.

No stock or sector is guaranteed to increase or decline in any situation due to the multiple factors and variables involved that may affect company performance.

Car Industry

The car industry is often a good barometer of what is going on in the economy.

This is due to the fact that when things are going well people want to treat themselves to new vehicles.

When things are slowing down, people do not want to take on large debt and monthly expenses.

If you notice that car sales are slowing down, then this could be a sign of things going on in the wider economy.

You may remember when President Obama did the "cash for clunkers" initiative some years back.

Although this was touted as an environmental program, rest assured, it was also to help the car industry to recover from the 08/09 situation.

Car companies rely on many suppliers for parts and materials to build their cars.

During the 80/09 situation, they were hit extremely hard.

This caused many companies to lay off workers etc.

Which is obviously bad for local economies where the businesses were based, but also the broader economy.

The "cash for clunkers" program gave the industry a kickstart, and by default, was of benefit to the broader economy.

It also instilled confidence in consumers as they saw lots of brand-new cars on the road.

As always, take into account factors such as a company may have released a model that the public is not keen on or they may have had a lot of recalls that gained negative press.

Be sure to do some adequate research.

However, if a company is usually booming and is starting to slow down suddenly, then it may be a case of people tightening their belts due to economic pressures.

Larger car company stocks may sink quite heavily during an economic downturn, but they are usually robust enough to recover over time.

It all depends on the individual company and the financial situation they face.

If we do endure economic turmoil before or during the transition to new digital currencies, and that leads to a bad recession or depression, then you may see a lot of cars getting repossessed or sold off as individuals try to make ends meet or reduce monthly expenditures.

Bear in mind that in this scenario, the "almost new" second-hand market would be flooded with vehicles.

This could possibly affect new car sales and therefore the revenue and stock prices of car sector companies.

Also, take note that any companies that rely on them to buy supplies and materials from them would also be affected.

If you have stock in one of these companies and you notice things taking a downturn, you should be very aware that if they rely on a large car manufacturer for their business, their stock could be taking a downturn along with the manufacturer.

On the flip side.

If you know a certain company supplies parts etc to a large manufacturer and you see that the manufacturer is starting to trend upwards due to sales volume…

Also, although most car manufacturers take a tumble in an economic downturn, they often climb back in line with the economy as it recovers.

Financial Sector.

This is banking stocks, credit card stocks, loan companies, etc.

Obviously, if the economy is doing badly, so do financial companies.

As we all know, banks and other financial institutions are heavily invested in the loan business via car loans, mortgages, business loans, etc.

If the economy starts taking a downturn, then people start to struggle to pay and defaults start to occur.

As the world learned the hard way in 2008, if too many people default at once it seriously impacts the wider economy.

It causes a lack of confidence across the board.

Consumers, companies, and financial institutions all distrust each other.

It also causes liquidity problems as capital is lost via defaults and the money that is available is held very tightly rather than invested or borrowed.

If you see trouble in the loan markets and financial sector in general, it is almost always a sign of huge trouble in the economy.

If history is our teacher, then it tells us clearly that financial stocks get hit very hard during a recession/crash.

It may be something to give consideration to if the market bottoms prior to or during the digital currency transition.

Some banks and institutions may fail, many did in the 2008 situation, including some of the biggest names in the financial world at that time.

But, as with any sector, some will recover and eventually boom again.

Financial sector stocks tend to have a lot further to drop in value, but also, therefore, have a larger potential for upside on the return journey back to the top.

Each company has its own nuances and factors involved.

One thing to give careful consideration to is that when the new digital currencies are introduced, there is most likely going to be payment processing companies involved.

I'm not going to name any, but, when you use your debit cards now to use funds straight from your own account, are there other companies involved besides your bank and the place of business you are paying?

I'm sure you have at least a rough idea of the types of companies I'm talking about.

If their stocks tank, rest assured, after the transition to the new digital currencies, when cash is gone, they will soar if they are involved in processing every single transaction in the world.

At the moment they are not involved in cash transactions.

But, if there is no cash and everything is digital and through the financial system in the same way as debit and credit cards are now…

If we do have a huge financial event and the old currencies are phased out to make way for the new digital ones, then these companies may initially take some serious hits on their stock prices.

But, once everything is settled and the transition is complete, if they are involved in processing the new currency transaction, their stock may become extremely interesting…

I'll let you put the pieces together on that for yourself.

Energy Sector.

This is composed of industries such as oil, gas, electricity etc.

Each one has its own aspects to consider but in the event of financial turmoil, they all tend to be impacted.

For example, if there are a lot of foreclosures on homes in an area, then you have to take into consideration the fact that it will impact the local power company.

Empty homes are not consuming electricity and therefore producing revenue for the power company.

If there are a lot of foreclosures, this also can be an indicator that there are outstanding unpaid power bills.

This is of course company revenue that has not been collected for a service rendered.

This impacts the power company on their quarterly earnings statements and can possibly influence the stock price negatively as investors see the issues via profitability for the company.

Gas is a similar story, as empty homes are not being heated and the factors above paint a similar story for that industry.

A lot of people do not realize that oil is not just used in the fuel industry via gasoline and other transport-related products.

Oil is used in a huge variety of everyday products such as furniture, clothes, hygiene products, and literally 1000's of other items.

It is actually quite surprising.

Do some research into what kind of products use petroleum in their manufacturing process as a component.

You may be shocked.

Because of its widespread applications in manufacturing, an economic slowdown impacts this sector far beyond fuel consumption.

Typically, unless geopolitical situations, such as war or instability in certain regions, apply pressure to production and drive up the price, oil prices are heavily impacted by the decreased demand.

This of course is a downward pressure on company stock prices.

As always, once things settle and people start to consume more, the price of oil rises and takes the stock prices with it.

A point to consider is that the global oil trade is currently conducted in the U.S dollar.

The "Petro Dollar" as it is known.

If the US dollar keeps getting printed at the rate it is, and other countries have already announced their planned move to their own digital currencies as I mentioned earlier.

How will this affect the dollar's status in this matter?

Will the oil trade move to another type of digital currency?

Or will the US have to launch a digital dollar in order to retain its status in the oil trading market?

Yet something else for you to consider is what I have mentioned about the old currencies being phased out and the new digital currencies being brought in.

If Russia, China, and the Eurozone, are already quite open about what they are doing, then do you not think that the U.S has got similar plans?

Remember what I said about the seemingly reckless abandon when it comes to pumping the current currencies, especially the dollar, into circulation?

It is highly unlikely the United States are going to want to lose their petrodollar status.

If the rest of the world's major currencies are going digital…

Some food for thought.

R.E.I.T.

Real Estate Investment Trusts invest in real estate in various forms.

There are various stocks for Residential and Commercial estate.

Each has its own pros and cons of course.

They can be a decent indicator of what is going on in the broader picture according to the situation.

Obviously, each stock can go up or down based on a variety of factors, such as debt levels and earnings, not just the sector they are based in.

In the event of a financial downturn, stocks like these can take a serious decline in value.

However, if they are in a good position and have the financial ability, they can acquire a lot of cheap real estate when a recession or crash occurs.

This has the potential to give them a good footing when things start to uptick and possibly boom at a later date.

Things to consider at this stage, and moving forward, is that most of these companies tend to hold the real estate long term as rentals.

They may make some comparatively short-term ventures, but generally, they tend to hold and rent.

As you may recall, earlier I mentioned that there are large amounts of people who are not paying rent and cannot be evicted due to government moratoriums.

It stands to reason that some of these companies are sitting with a backlog of unpaid rent from tenants who are still occupying their properties.

These properties are not earning money and will either have to rely on the tenants to pay them back over time, take them through the courts to get payment in the future, or wait until the moratoriums to expire so they can evict them and put in paying tenants.

Now, this is not to say these companies are in dire straits because of this.

But it's something for you to consider if you are interested in this kind of stock.

Now, if we do end up having another lockdown and/or an economic downturn of significant proportions and more businesses struggle, lay people off etc, then will this cause even more people to not be able to pay rent in the future?

Will there be another moratorium to cover those people?

Also, if we have a severe enough downturn, lots of urban areas will have economic and social issues due to unemployment and crime.

Will this affect the value of the properties these companies hold, and will they be able to charge the rates of rent they have done in the past if the area is less desirable?

All factors to consider when investing in such stocks.

On the other hand.

Let's say these stocks take a price tumble in the future due to those factors and real estate crashed like in 08/09.

Companies such as these who have sufficient capital on hand can go in and buy up swathes of bargain-priced properties that will eventually go up in value and also rent rates as the economy recovers.

As I said, I'm not naming any specific stocks in any of these sectors.

I'm trying to get you to think differently than most of these new "shoeshine" investors.

Do you think any of those people are thinking in these terms?

They are too busy waiting for another "Bitcointothemoon" tweet to show up in their feed for their investing strategy.

This is why I wrote this book.

Not to claim I'm an expert or to give financial blueprints.

Simply to get the reader to think and separate themselves from the masses.

As I said earlier, there are huge swathes of "investors" both in stocks and crypto, who think they know what they are doing because they made some money on the back of trending tweets.

Rest assured, take most of them off social media and just give them trading screens, stocks or crypto, and tell them to repeat their magic moves.

You will get a lot of "deer in the headlights" expressions.

If I am right about what I think is coming up, as I have described through this book, they had better hope their trending hashtags guide them in the right direction.

Because if not, they will follow the herd right off the financial cliff if those hashtags are wrong.

It wouldn't be the first time.

Hence why I want my readers to think for themselves and not base their investing or any financial matters on hashtags.

Luxury

In an economic event, certain areas, such as luxury item companies, can often be the first to drop in price and one of the last to recover.

It's really simple logic as to why.

If money is tight and income is not guaranteed to be secure in the future, people tend to cut back on spending needlessly.

Luxury items by definition are not a necessity in life, they are a luxury.

So certain companies and sectors are liable to have a notable dip in earnings until things recover and people are able and comfortable enough to start splurging on luxury items.

This is not to say that these companies are hot potatoes that you should jump out of at the first sign of trouble.

These companies are global now, so even though one region of the world may be in recession.

Another region may be a golden goose for them that fills the gaps in earnings.

Again, as always, do your research into trends via matching historical stock price and earnings reports against dates when recessions were happening in the past.

I believe this next financial event is going to be global, so I personally believe that the impact will be more along the lines of a crash than a slowdown.

Luxury can be a type of canary in the mine of sorts.

Now, this is far from foolproof, but give it some consideration for a moment.

If luxury companies suddenly report drops in earnings, then, typically this means that those who usually spend, are not.

This can be because things are tight across the board, or that they know something is brewing in the economy.

Most wealthy people are business owners and/or investors.

If they are not spending on luxury goods, enough for it to affect the industry revenue and stock prices, then either their businesses are slowing down and/or they have heard about, or can see, problems in the wider economy.

Again, not foolproof by any stretch of the imagination, but something to consider.

Also, it's no secret that it's not just the wealthy who buy luxury goods.

There are plenty of people of average to decent economic standing who buy luxury goods.

Not everyone who buys an expensive watch or purse is a millionaire upwards.

So, if these companies are reporting low earnings and stocks are dipping, then it can also mean that various economic class levels are tightening their belts and not splurging.

Again, it is not typically your factory worker or restaurant employee who is buying these luxury items.

It is business owners, small or otherwise, and investors, small or otherwise.

If all of these types of people are not purchasing, or at least not in sufficient numbers…

Something may be coming down the economic pipe.

Luxury can possibly be a good buy at the bottom, because as I said, the economy will at some stage boom again.

It's just baked into the cake for us to have ups and downs.

Luxury stocks may possibly rise again in the future so long as the individual company survives the downtimes.

Some luxury companies have been in business for centuries and have endured through World Wars and various other global events that crushed other companies and industries.

But nothing is guaranteed.

Security Sector

What I think is going to be a huge growth sector in the coming years is home, commercial, and personal security.

Let's be honest.

The streets in most urban centers these days are not becoming more tranquil or safe.

In fact, crime in some cities has spiked since the lockdowns were eased.

The causes of this can be varied and far too broad to be discussed here, but, one thing to consider is that a lot of people are now short on money through losing their jobs.

Some areas have taken softer stances on certain crimes in relation to this, but that is, again, too broad a topic to discuss here.

The point of the matter is that many businesses and individuals are getting increasingly concerned about the security of themselves, their businesses, and their homes.

I honestly see these problems getting worse over time, and if we do have a serious economic event or another lockdown that causes further job losses, I expect these problems to grow at a rapid pace over a short time frame.

This will mean serious potential growth for security guard companies, CCTV companies, personal protection item companies, alarm companies, so on and so forth.

This is something you should give consideration to.

Not only on a national scale but also on a local scale.

If you know that certain companies have franchises in your area, and the demand for that companies products and services is liable to go through the roof due to rising crime in the area, then consider this.

If the franchise does really well, then that will knock on to the parent company's success.

If that company is based in many hotspots that are experiencing upticks in demand due to rising crime etc, then the company on the whole may have some great earnings quarters.

If you can see this coming, then consider taking a look at their stock, and the stock of any equipment suppliers they may use, ahead of time.

Don't spread yourself too thin.

There are plenty of other sectors you can consider looking at.

As I have said multiple times, I am not trying to give a financial blueprint.

I'm trying to get my readers to think differently to the masses.

Especially the hashtag crowd.

If you look at what I have written, you will see the threads of logic that can be applied to sectors in order to make money, before, during, and after, any economic event we may have coming our way.

In my experience, the key to investing is to specialize in certain sectors and become as versed as you can with them.

What triggers price rises, falls, and even companies to go bust in those sectors.

I don't advise sticking to one or two, but I personally find that between 5 and 7 sectors is a good working frame for me.

It all depends on what is going on.

If I have less than 5 then I risk missing out on other opportunities.

If I have too many, then I'm spread too thin on keeping up on news within those sectors and risk missing out on opportunities or even getting stung and taking a loss, because I wasn't giving adequate attention to the sector.

You may think differently, but that practice has served me well over the years.

This is not to say you shouldn't invest in a sector that suddenly becomes hot if there is potential for profit, but, just make sure it has not become hot due to the hashtag crowd.

GameStop is a prime example.

The second bit of advice I will give you is this.

Invest based on logic, not emotion.

Don't get drawn into hype and invest based on the enthusiasm of yourself and others.

But also don't avoid an investment out of fear or the fears of others.

The hype is of course a direct nod back to the hashtag crowd, but I've said more than enough on that at this point.

Fear may be because you have seen potential in a stock, but have not seen anyone else talking about it, or have heard a lot of naysaying.

Let me give you a story from my investing moves to illustrate my point.

I will not name the stock directly, but you will get my point.

I saw a stock in an emerging industry.

I read that they were attracting investors and spending heavily in infrastructure etc.

Not rumors, factual-based research.

So I decided to put a few grand into this companies stock.

I mentioned this to a few friends of mine who also invest, and they were apprehensive and even flat out against investing in this stock.

I had my own pangs of fear develop based on talking to them.

But, I stayed logical, and thought,

"OK, they have raised substantial amounts of money from professional investors. These experts can see potential enough to throw huge amounts of money at them. That is good enough for me"

A few weeks later the stock shot up and I made substantial gains then sold off.

Just around the time I was getting ready to sell, the hashtag crowd got wind of the stock and piled in.

Bear in mind, they were several weeks behind other investors such as me who got in at far lower prices.

The stock surged and I sold out at a handsome profit, because I suspected the hashtag crowd would get in and pump and dump the stock.

I was correct.

My friends either kicked themselves for letting fear stop them investing or got in way later than I did on the back of hashtags and made modest gains in comparison.

I think it was a year or so later, the stock was very low again.

Not quite pennies, but about a third of its hashtag highs.

I read from reliable articles etc, that the company had some moves coming up with investors and potential product collaborations with other companies.

Again, I told my friends that I was going in and that they should read up about the company to see what they thought.

Some again balked that "Lightning doesn't strike twice"

One or two listened to me, read up, and decided to get into the stock.

A few weeks later it was steadily creeping up and the hashtag crowd got involved.

I knew then that I would sell off on a certain day when the hype was reaching fever pitch.

I did, very early in the trading session, and made 84% gains on my investment.

I put in 5 figures of capital, so as you can imagine, that was a nice payday.

By the end of the day, as I recall, the stock had dropped notably.

Still the hashtag crowd was continuing the chorus.

The next day was a continuation of its price decline, until it eventually returned to less than I paid for it in the first place, well ahead of the hype.

I saw online there were a lot of "bagholders" that got in at the highs of the main day and were grieved when it had dropped by significant amounts over the following days.

Moral of the story.

Do your research, and don't let the fear or hype of others override your research.

If you have notable and reliable people, even friends, who state good cases against investing in something, then take notice and make your own decision.

But, if your research is indicating possible gains or losses, then do not let the fear of others and definitely not the hype crowd, push you into, or away from, an investment you have researched to your own satisfaction.

This is why I say pick a select few sectors and become very versed in them.

Do not base your investing on hype and hashtags.

Now don't get me wrong.

The reason I know this is because in my early investing days, I got caught up in the hashtag hype trap and lost all of the capital that I invested into a stock.

Around $13k to be exact.

I won't name the company or industry, but the story is as follows.

I had bounced in and out of a volatile stock and made a few k.

I was loving it as I was new to investing.

At one point, I took my attention off this stock and industry because, being a noob, I was chasing some other hyped stock and sector.

I missed out on significant gains I would have made on that stock if I had been paying attention.

This, of course, was like a red rag to a bull as a new hyped investor.

I started to keep eye on this stock for any rumors of another surge in price.

It didn't take long before the hashtags and rumors started.

I jumped in for $13k.

The hashtaggers were backing it, I couldn't go wrong.

The stock started to dip.

I got nervous.

#buythedip was rampant.

"It'll be OK, it'll fly up and I'll cash out" I thought.

It kept going down over the next few days.

I then had lost about 40% so I felt I just needed it to have a mini-surge so I could at least pull a decent amount back out and just take a little loss.

Within days the company announced bankruptcy and the stock was frozen.

Couldn't sell out and it was priced at zero now anyway.

That was that.

All through, until the official news of the bankruptcy, #buythedip was rampant.

There my friends is a cautionary tale and one of the main reasons I advise massively against basing your investing on hype and hashtags.

I just see it as a learning experience.

Was I grieved at the time and did I feel stupid?

Absolutely!

But now, I'm so glad I went through that experience because now I invest the way I do.

I have not lost any money of note, nothing more than a percent or two, since.

But I have made plenty of double-digit percentage gain moves since I changed my mindset.

I have also watched person after person become bagholders on the same stocks I profited from, purely because they followed the hashtag crowd.

Do your research and become proficient in a select number of sectors.

Don't let hype or fear guide your investing.

Invest and wait to exploit the hashtag crowds, don't wait for them to tell you what to buy.

Buy it ahead of time and sell it to them later at a profit while the hashtag hype is in full swing.

It's their decision to base their investing moves that way.

So they profit or loss as they may.

Not my problem.

Not your problem.

That is how the game is played.

Gold and Silver

Typically, during a financial crisis there is an uptick, and sometimes surge, in the price of what are known as safe-havens.

Examples of these are gold and silver.

Gold is where governments and large financial institutions tend to "hedge their bets" as they say.

Once the price surges it tends to cause a surge in silver price as people who cannot afford gold, or have trouble finding actual physical to purchase, instead turn to silver.

Now, here are a few things to consider.

There are various regulations that vary from region to region with regards to the purchase, holding, and selling of bullion.

It is imperative that you do your own research on the matter and become versed in the topic with regards to your region etc.

As always, it may be beneficial to consult a professional in this field.

There are variations in tax situations from place to place and it is imperative that you stay on the right side of the law at all times.

You do not want to get yourself in a bind due to ignorance.

Better to stay out of the matter than get yourself into situations that could be averted with some research and professional consultation. I prefer mining stocks over physical bullion, but everyone has different standpoints.

In the event of a recession, and especially a crash scenario, there is potential for profits via bullion.

Whether physical or paper-based.

But it is not guaranteed, so there is also the chance of losses.

As always, do your research and consult a professional before investing a penny.

Real Estate.

Real estate, both commercial and residential, can suffer greatly in a financial downturn.

As you would imagine it is caused by defaults on mortgages and commercial suffers due to businesses closing and therefore the lack of rental income.

I mentioned REIT in its own section due to it being stock-based.

Here I am referring to actual real-world property as opposed to investing in funds etc.

When a market has bottomed, the potential in real estate is not to be sniffed at.

Buildings can drop significantly in price and provide rental income opportunities as the economy recovers.

They also provide the opportunity for significant profits, when sold, when the market booms again in the future.

As we have seen along the way through this book, there is a lot of potential for profits in a recession/crash by buying distressed assets and later reselling them when the market recovers and returns to higher prices.

The beauty of real estate is that it can provide income in the meantime via rental money.

I am not a real estate professional, so, therefore, I strongly advise you to do a lot of serious research and consult professionals before even considering putting a penny into any investments.

It is, however, worth mentioning as an area to consider looking at in the event of a recession/crash.

As I write this, the real estate prices are surging.

There are no major floods of defaults, evictions, or foreclosures of any sort currently that I'm aware of.

I do, however, see this as just a matter of time.

As I write this, the eviction moratorium ends very soon…

Again, this is just personal speculation, but I don't see a rosy future for commercial real estate when the crash hits.

Many large stores didn't pay rent during the outbreak and lockdown.

I assume most paid it back as we moved along, but it doesn't give me a lot of faith that when the crash hits they will be more prone to come up with rent than in the lockdown.

If a lot of stores pull out of malls it can be devastating not only for the mall, but the local community.

People tend to work as close to home as they can.

If the malls start losing stores, then people will start losing their jobs, both at the stores and at the mall itself.

Malls with lots of empty storefronts do not tend to fare well with foot traffic as no one wants to go to a "ghost mall"

This in turn knocks on to the remaining stores and so the cycle goes.

Also, if a lot of people who live in the area around the mall have lost their jobs, then the area may lose its shine, to put it nicely.

Rest assured, few people like to go through economically distressed areas and shop at a mall full of empty stores.

Judging by the number of people who would potentially lose their jobs in the crash, I suspect retail stores are in for a potentially bleak future.

Combine that with the rise in online shopping, and if I'm right about an uptick in crime resulting from economic hardship from the crash, it's not looking rosy at all, in my opinion.

If the crash is as severe as I think it will be, then a lot of companies will close or at least layoff workers to reduce their overheads.

There are going to be a lot of people unable to pay their rent or mortgage in the coming future.

This, if severe enough, can, and probably will in my opinion, knock heavily on to the residential real estate sector.

If it does, it will not only knock on to the financial sectors such as banks, credit cards, and car loans, but also companies that provide household goods and services.

There are not going to be many people shopping for new couches or bathroom overhauls if they have lost their job or are being kicked out by the bank or landlord.

There may be stock buying opportunities in those sectors.

Because although a bust always follows a boom, a boom will always occur at some point after a bust.

The economy will recover, and take stocks back up with it at some point.

We will see how this pans out, as it is still relatively early days.

Convertible Assets

This is something you should put into consideration.

If they do, and I strongly suspect they will, offer a low exchange rate from the old currencies into the new digital ones to prevent the inflation from carrying over, then you will want to have some of your current wealth in convertible assets.

This is an asset that will retain or recover its value in the new digital currency.

This may be a stock of a company that is here to stay no matter what happens, bullion, or perhaps, maybe, certain digital coins.

A large company, I'm not naming any, will weather the financial crisis and recover afterwards.

Its stock may drop massively in a crash, but will recover over time.

Denominated and traded in the new digital currency when the markets reopen after the transition.

So, if you time it correctly, you can buy up lots of valuable stocks at cut-rate prices as the market tanks.

As everyone is cashing out into old currencies to have cash on hand, you can be dumping that currency and buying up valuable company stocks at firesale prices.

Not only are you hopefully avoiding any low exchange rate in the digital transition, you are also acquiring assets that can recover greatly in price as time goes on.

Denominated in the new digital currency.

You may also discover that some companies who usually offer dividend payments will suspend their dividends as the crisis unfolds.

This has the potential to drive their price down further.

But, when things start to recover, they could possibly resume dividend payments to attract investors and also because it is part of their business's financial structure.

I'm sure you can see what I'm getting at.

It could be a golden opportunity to sweep up large amounts of dividend stocks that will not only go up in value over time but also pay you money to own them.

To give an example.

We will use the old currencies at the moment because we do not know how the digital rate will convert etc, so let's keep it simple for now to illustrate the concept.

Let's say stock A is currently $20 during this mania and pays a $2 dividend.

This is a 10% dividend.

10% of $20 = $2

For example's sake, let's say the stock tanks to $10 in the crash and suspends the dividend.

You could go in and buy up the stock at $10 for each unit.

Now, let's say things settle and the stock stays at $10 for a while and then resumes the dividend at say $12 stock price.

Investors would be interested and start getting back into the stock driving its price back up.

Let's say it recovers to $20 again.

The dividend has been reinstated at $2 and is 10% of the $20 again.

Not for you.

You only paid $10 a stock, so your dividend is equal to 20%.

$2 = 20% of $10.

So, let's say 1000 units, 2 investors.

Investor A pays $10,000 for 1000 units at the market bottom.

Investor B pays $20,000 for 1000 units at the market top.

Both get a $2 dividend per stock owned.

$2 x 1000 units = $2000 per year dividend total.

Investor A has invested $10.000 to earn $2000 per year.

Investor B has invested $20,000 to earn $2000 per year.

Plus investor A has made $10,000 on stock price increase now the stock has returned to its $20 price.

See my point?

You don't only have to do this on dividend stocks of course, any decent stock will recover and you can aim to make your money by selling them later when the price recovers.

But personally, I like the sound of acquiring as many dividend stocks as I can so I can build up a yearly dividend cash flow…

How about you?

Also, when the stock has reinstated the dividend with the aim of the overall price recovery, this means dividend money can be reinvested to buy the stock on it's way back up.

$12.

$14.

Sure the percentage will work out as lower, but the $2 payment is still being acquired for cheaper than $20.

A $2 dividend on a $15 stock is still a very good rate.

So, give that concept some thought, and if you are interested, then do your research and consult a professional before making any investments.

But I'm sure you can see why I like that concept.

As for other convertible assets, well, there is of course bullion.

Bullion is its own beast, and, as always, you will need to do your research and seek professional advice, but, consider this.

If the old currencies go wild with inflation, gold and silver will typically become a hedge.

People will buy them because the inflation carries over into their price.

But, unlike crypto coins, bullion is unlikely to be banned, and will most likely hold some kind of value versus the new digital currency.

Is that guaranteed?

Absolutely not.

Private ownership of bullion in the United States was banned at one stage in 1933.

Bear in mind, this was not long after the 1929 crash in the scheme of things.

The great depression was in full swing.

The ban was based on the logic that people were hoarding wealth in bullion and therefore not spending and hindering the recovery from the recession.

Could this happen again?

Maybe, but I personally doubt it.

I can't guarantee it won't, but, I see it as unlikely.

Again, you need to do your own research and come to your own conclusions as to if bullion is a good idea, but it is a convertible asset and so therefore I have included it here.

According to how fast the conversion happens and how things transpire, it may be possible to buy up lots of distressed real estate.

These can recover in price later, but also provide income via rent in the meantime.

In the last real estate crash, investors were buying up foreclosed homes for cash and then renting them out.

Homes that were selling for $500k were being scooped up for $150k in some cases.

I heard far more extreme cases here in Vegas.

Condos that were selling for $250k were scooped up for $40k etc.

Put it that way.

But, if we are going into a digital transition, I do not know how the timeline and window of opportunity to turn old currency into distressed real estate will pan out.

Plus it will require cash on hand.

Banks are unlikely to be loaning money out at the time of the crash.

Again, just a concept for you to consider, research, and come to your own conclusions on.

There are other types of convertible assets but for now, I will end with crypto coins.

As I said earlier, I am of the firm mind that coins with anonymous ledgers will be banned once the official digital currencies are either launched, or close to launch.

It may be afterward, but I believe they will be banned at some stage.

I have described why, so I will focus on the matter at hand.

It is possible, who knows at this point, that the current coins without anonymous ledgers may be allowed to coexist with the new digital currencies.

I think they will, but obviously cannot do more than speculate at this point.

How will their price react etc?

I simply do not know.

But, it may be worth considering that if you are in Bitcoin and its cohorts such as Dogecoin, that when they hit a price you are happy with, cashing out and using the money to buy up some of the coins you think may survive the cull.

The reason is, if they ban the financial institutions from taking payments from crypto platforms as they get rid of the old currencies and ban Bitcoin and co, then, possibly, you may be able to park your old currency in the surviving coins, if timed correctly.

If they do survive, then you may be able to convert them into the new digital currencies if and when they lift the restrictions on the trading platforms.

See my point?

As you can see, there is a LOT of speculation and "ifs" and "maybes" involved.

I have no idea how that will all pan out and neither does anyone else.

Especially the hashtaggers etc.

You will have to do your own research and come to your own conclusions on that.

I merely introduce the concept for your consideration.

An idea, nothing more.

I may or may not look at that route for my own investing.

But at this stage, I am still heavily researching and pondering.

I personally am more interested in the stock aspect.

But I'm not ruling out the above concept to take advantage of any surges in crypto as the hashtaggers pile in as a "hedge"

I will decide as I go along and things unfold.

So there you have the concept of convertible assets.

There are others.

You may notice that the wealthy buy up art and rare memorabilia for outrageous prices.

Yet more types of convertible assets.

But I know nothing of either, so I won't be investing in those types of assets.

I mention them to further illustrate the concept.

With some research and thought, you may discover other types of convertible assets to your liking.

All the best and as always, do your research and consult professionals before parting with a penny on any investment.

Becoming Self Employed

I mentioned earlier about aiming to become financially independent ASAP.

This can be achieved via dividend payments and investing in stocks as a trader or perhaps starting your own business, but being your own boss and creating your own financial independence takes a certain mindset and a set of traits.

If you have never been your own boss, you may have certain ideas about how it runs.

You may think that it's great because you can do what you want all day and do not have to answer to anyone.

True, to a certain point.

But, doing what you want all day should be centered around making money and not lounging around just because you can.

You also DO have to answer to someone.

Yourself.

You have to be the boss you need, not the boss you want.

If you know you have certain bad traits, such as procrastination or getting up late in the day, guess what?

You need to eliminate them.

Not keep them in check.

Eliminate them.

So, no matter if you aim to be a person that builds their fortune from investing, or one that builds their own business, or a combination, you are going to have to get yourself in line.

In this next section, we will look at what I have learned being self-employed with a combination of investing and online business ventures.

This is not theory, it is based on experience.

TRAITS AND MINDSET

In this section, we will look at some very important aspects.

Traits and Mindset.

In order to be self-employed, you need to have these aspects.

Desire and Clarity of Purpose.

You need to have an overwhelming desire to succeed at your chosen goals.

You have to put it at the center of your life.

It has to be an obsession where the discomfort of the challenges are dwarfed by the sheer burning desire to achieve it.

The desire has to be strong enough to carry you through all of the hard work and highs and lows of being an entrepreneur.

Rest assured. You will have both in abundance.

Especially at the beginning, long before any results are even visible on the horizon.

If you do not desire the outcome to the degree that enables you to endure discomfort, then you will not achieve your goals.

It is as simple as that.

Apply it to any venture you undertake.

Investing, business, you need to have the will to succeed.

Perhaps you want to start a blog and promote affiliate offers.

You need to be ready to sit at your computer for many hours, with little or no financial rewards, for extended periods of time.

Days will run into weeks and months.

You may succeed, or you may fail, at the end of it all.

You may start and snowball into massive success within months.

But, you will not find out until you have done all the hard groundwork.

Setting up the blog, adding content, and building a social media following.

Many more aspects go into that business model, I assure you.

Hours upon hours of groundwork.

I'm not talking twenty or thirty hours.

I'm talking, if you are serious about setting up a stable consistent income, hundreds of hours.

Some tasks are fun every time.

Others are a chore the first time around, but still need to be done, hour after hour.

Week after week.

Potentially indefinitely on some aspects.

All without financial return in the beginning, and nothing guaranteed long term.

You had better ensure you have a desire.

An obsession with achieving your goals.

You have to know what you want and refuse to allow yourself to stop until you have achieved this.

As self-employed, you have to be able to do this alone.

No one is pushing you.
No one is encouraging you.
You are accountable to yourself.

If you do not make it happen, then it does not happen.

Again, I mention self-discipline and self-motivation.

They are core traits.

Absolute core.

In order for you to keep this desire strong, you have to know what you want and how you are going to do it, as I described earlier.

This is clarity of purpose.

Why and how.

You cannot have vague goals backed by scattered, ill-thought-out, plans.

You need to know in absolute certainty.

"This is what I have to do in order to attain what I want."

No ifs, buts, or maybes.

"This is what I have to do in order to attain what I want."

Then do it, and don't stop until you achieve your goal.

Your next task is to tie your goal to your chosen way of making income and road map your way to your goal.

For example.

You may do something along these lines.

Your goal is to replace your job income of $60k.

You decide to write e-books and price them to make $5 per copy.

Income target is $5k a month.

So, $5000 divided by $5 = 1000 books a month.

Your goal is 1000 books a month to reach your $5k a month desired income.

Your first task is to plan out your roadmap.

This will be your clarity of purpose.

Research and plan your book.

Write and edit your book ready for launch.

Set up your blog.

Set up payment facilities to handle purchases of your e-book.

Set up your mailing list.

Set up your social media presence.

Interlink and optimize the blog, social media, and mailing list.

Upload your book ready for promotion and sales.

Start adding content to your blog on a consistent basis.

Promote your book every day on social media and weekly via your mailing list.

That is a very basic road map to illustrate my point.

Your daily financial goal is 1000 divided by 30 = 33.33 books per day.

Call it 34 books a day.

Your daily goals may look something like this.

2 blog posts.

20 Social Media Posts.

1000 words towards next book.

You will do this day after day with the aim to sell 34 books each day.

You have your overall goal of $5k a month to quit your job.

(Your Desire.)

You have your 34 books a day target and the planned structure to achieve it.

(Your clarity of purpose)

In order to carry yourself through this, you need the next traits.

Focus and Commitment.

Two other traits you need are focus and commitment.

Your focus has to be dominated by your goals.

This is why your desire is so important.

If your desire is so strong, it becomes an obsession, then your focus will follow.

Your efforts and actions always directly follow what your attention/focus is on.

If your desire is centered on leveling up a character in a video game, then rest assured, your focus will be there guiding your actions and commitment.

The more you desire and obsess over leveling, the more you will focus on attaining it.

You will commit your time and actions to playing the game.

Your business should be carried by that same desire, focus, and commitment.

Your actions will then follow.

This is the fuel to the engine of success.

If you obsess and focus your actions on leveling your character, eventually you will get there.

Your business is absolutely no different.

You may be thinking:

"Well, what if my business doesn't provide the income I want or fails?"

Then restructure your plans.

Your desire is the same.

You still want that $5k a month.

That is the key aspect.

You can always change course slightly to avoid obstacles.

It doesn't mean you have to change your destination altogether or abandon ship!

Seeking to be creative, and being able to adapt to problems, is integral to being self-employed and will be covered later in its own section.

You need to be able to change with the ebb and flow of business.

It's not optional.

However, if you have researched your plans thoroughly before enacting them, then it should be a case of adapting and evolving rather than scrapping them.

Your focus will highlight any problems as you go.

You cannot dabble in something, expect it to be plain sailing, and to be on top of your game.

If you are laser-focused on your business, then naturally, you will know it inside out.

The good, bad, ugly, boring, amazing, productive, unproductive.

You will know it all.

As with anything, experience makes you more competent in anything you do.

The more you do it, the better you become.

This is why commitment is also a core aspect.

Focus all of your attention.

Commit your time and actions towards building your business in order to achieve your goal and therefore desire.

To laser target your focus, take your plan structure, your roadmap, and move along step by step.

When you reach your next step in your plan, that is your focus.

Nothing else.

You commit to completing that step until it is done.

You do not bounce from step to step because you are bored or more interested in another aspect.

Focus and commit to working on it until it is done to satisfaction.

If you catch yourself losing focus, then take a minute to see what is dominating your attention.

Whatever it is, eliminate it until you have completed the thing you are supposed to be focused on.

If it is your phone, then turn it off, or at least put it out of reach if you need it on for important calls etc.

If it is the T.V. in the background, then turn it off.

If other people in your home are noisy, then go out of the room and work somewhere else.

If that is not possible, go to the library and work on your laptop there.

Allow nothing and no one, unless of course it really is important, to distract you from what you are doing.

If you were on a video game, then you would be quick to tune people out or tell them to leave you alone.

Your business is far more important than any video game.

Do not focus on leveling your character up and getting better gear.

Focus on leveling yourself up and getting a better life!

A simple way to remember this concept is the following phrase.

"Focus on the task at hand until it is complete."

Write it down and put it on a posted note on your monitor.

Anytime you find yourself getting distracted, sooner or later you will see that note and get back on track.

Assuming you have self-discipline and self-motivation of course.

Notice how I keep bringing up certain traits and applying them to aspects of being an entrepreneur?

It's because they are so important.

I'm drawing your focus to them and trying to encourage you to commit to those values.

In order to know whether, and to what degree, you have those traits, we need to look at the next two traits in this section.

Know yourself and your habits.

If you are aiming to be self-employed, then you need to know yourself and your habits.

What I mean by this, is that you need to take careful self-assessment of yourself, and what causes you to act the way you do.

Your strengths and weaknesses.

If you find yourself getting distracted or procrastinating, then you need to realize that, establish why you do it, and what triggers it.

If you know that you work better in the morning, then you should realize this and seek to capitalize upon it.

At the moment, for some reason, I find that I write with more focus after around 10 am.

I get up between 6 am and 7 am every single day.

Bear in mind I have no job schedule, so no one is forcing me up at those times.

I literally can rot in bed till I say different.

But that's why I have to have self-motivation and discipline.

When I was a teenager, I would get up any time after 2 pm if I wasn't at school and enforced by a schedule to get up.

Most teenagers are the same.

Like most parents, my father used to berate me for it.

He was, and still is, up at 5 am most days.

He used to tell me how 6 am was the best part of the day.

I used to either laugh at him or grumble every single time I heard it.

I'll tell you what.

He was 100% correct.

I used to get up at this time or that time and everyone was already going through their day.

If I went to the store, it was packed with people, things were sold out, parking was an irritating experience on top of contending with traffic on the roads.

Now, I get up and if I need to run errands, I'm off as early as I can.

I currently live in Las Vegas, so a lot of grocery stores are open 24 hours a day.

I'm usually up at 6 am to eat, freshen up, etc.

By 7 am, I'm on my way to the grocery store.

By 8 am, I'm back at home with everything packed away.

I'm ready to start working on my business or to start my gym routine.

A lot of people haven't even got out of bed yet, and my errands are done.

Some errands have to be done at a later time of course.

A lot of stores here open around 10 am.

So, I'll do what I'm doing till around 9.45 am, then head out.

Here and there.

There and back.

Done.

Usually before 11 am, but certainly midday.

Traffic is just starting to pick up.

In summer, the heat is peaking, and people are aggravated and rushing around.

I head home to continue working.

If I want to go out to see friends, I wait until after 6 when the traffic has subsided.

My life is vastly less stressful.

Simply because I get up early so that I can get everything done before the masses attempt to.

"Okay great, so what has this got to do with know yourself and your habits?"

Simple.

I knew I used to be lazy about getting up.

It was a weakness of mine.

A hindrance.

This was caused by my ethics.

My ethic was simply, I didn't want to get up and wanted to delay doing things I didn't want to do.

So, I changed my ethic to "I want to get out of bed so I can get things done".

Sounds so simple, doesn't it?

It is.

Everything we do is based on conscious decisions, that are based around our subconscious, which is influenced by our ethics.

Someone can talk about going to the gym.

If they have a habit of lounging on the couch watching TV, then rest assured, their gym routine habit has a competitor that will win a portion of the time.

You need to eliminate bad habits and replace them with good ones.

Everything you do in life is a choice.

Not what happens to you, but what you choose to do.

This can apply to action or reaction.

It is all on you every day of your life.

You can blame whoever you want, for whatever you want.

It was your choice how you acted or reacted.

Never forget that.

You should aim to set yourself up for good habits.

Again, get yourself a pen and paper.

Sit and write down the habits you have that you know are holding you back.

Write down anything you perceive as detrimental to you.

Be honest with yourself.

You are doing this for you, no one else.

Some examples:

Procrastination.

Laziness.

Unfocused.

Never finish a task.

Watch too much TV.

Always late.

When you have done that, write down what you consider to be your good habits.

Do not write what you wish you did, only write what you already do habitually.

Some examples:

Always start what you finish.

Persist against the odds.

Go to the gym daily.

Read every day.

Now you have those in front of you, take a moment to consider that these habits are a direct result of your mindset, and also character traits.

If you do not like what is in front of you, then you need to change them.

No one is going to change them for you.

It's all on you.

Remember this, and remember it well,

Comfort is the enemy of progression.

That may sound very dramatic, but I assure you, that if you get in the habit of sleeping in just because you can, or avoiding things because you are comfy on the couch playing video games, you will fail.

I don't care if you are starting an online business, investing, or any other venture, if you allow yourself to form bad habits, you will fail.

I'm not saying live a life of discomfort, I'm saying do not allow seeking comfort to stand in the way of your success.

Stay hungry and focused.

If you achieve a goal, create another one.

If you do not feel like doing something that may make you money, but you are comfortable on the couch, exercise self-discipline and get up straight away to do it.

Become uncomfortable being comfortable.

Seek more for yourself.

Comfort is the enemy of progression.

Which brings us to the next section.

Self-Confidence and Self-Accountability

To survive and thrive as you build your own income, you have to possess the traits of self-confidence and self-accountability.

Self-confidence is needed because you will have to learn to believe in yourself when few, if any, people do.

When you first start hinting about becoming financially self-sufficient, you are going to be met with all kinds of opinions from those around you:

"You can't do that, it's too hard."

"What makes you think you are going to succeed?'

"Don't waste your time, it's rare anyone succeeds."

"That's cool, let me know how you get on."

"Good luck, so what are you thinking for dinner?"

The majority of people around you will be in one of 4 camps.

Against you doing it, out of concern you will fail.

Amused that you think you are capable.

Indifferent.

Supportive.

I assure you that the first three will be the most vocal and numerous.

So, it is crucial that you have self-confidence.

Without it, you will be hindering yourself and leaning towards failure every step of the way.

Do not confuse self-confidence with arrogance.

No one likes arrogance directed at them.

That much I assure you of.

You don't have to be humble to the point of appearing unconfident in yourself, but that is far better than being overconfident when dealing with detractors.

The only person who has to truly believe in you, is you.

Your success is not contingent on whether someone else thinks you can do it.

It is contingent on you believing in yourself and using that belief to fuel your actions.

The more you do, the better you will get at your chosen venture.

The better you get, the more competent you will feel.

The more competent you feel, the more confidence you will have in your abilities.

This positive loop will lead you to success.

So, you should make it imperative that you have self-confidence and use that to spur you into action.

To clear up something about other people's opinions, let me tell you this.

Most people will never attempt to be self-employed.

Simply because they do not have enough self-confidence in themselves to try.

These same people will also not want to see you outdo them.

I'm sorry, but it's true.

If you achieve financial independence, or even huge success, you will have made them feel even less confident in themselves.

Sounds odd?

It's true.

People are full of insecurities.

Fear and jealousy mostly.

If we simply look at fear and jealousy, I will prove my point.

They have inner fear they won't succeed, because they do not have self-confidence.

That is where fear comes from.

The belief that a situation is beyond the person's ability to succeed in.

Jealousy comes from the belief that they want it, but can't have it, so why should you?

Again, both are rooted in a lack of self-confidence.

If you have too much self-confidence, rest assured, they will label that as arrogance and feel belittled.

If you do not have enough self-confidence, they will see it as weakness and use that as an excuse to belittle or dismiss your plans.

Either way, they win, and you lose.

Self-confidence is exactly that.

Confidence in oneself, and for oneself.

You can appear neutral and still be very self-confident.

Again, I repeat, do not confuse a healthy degree of self-confidence with arrogance or over-confidence.

Both will lead you to failure.

Self-confidence will give you the courage to start your venture, and to see it through in the face of the adversity you WILL face.

Do not for one minute think the path will be easy.

It will not.

The people who tell you that it is are usually trying to sell you one of their courses.

"Just follow my course and it will be fine. You can't fail!"

Yes, you can.

But, the more you do something, the more competent you become.

As I described above.

Self-confidence leads to action.

It is contingent on you believing in yourself, and using that belief to fuel your actions.

The more you do, the better you will get at your chosen venture.

The better you get, the more competent you will feel.

The more competent you feel, the more confidence you will have in your abilities.

The more confidence you have in your abilities, the more you will repeat the actions that produced success.

This positive loop will lead you to success.

You have to have the self-confidence to start, but you also have to have a firm grip on reality that you are still new to your path.

Do not expect miracles overnight.

It is a well-worn cliché that has found itself on many internet memes.

"My overnight success took ten years."

This is true in almost all cases.

Sure, you will get people who blow up overnight.

It happens.

It could be you.

But.

Remember this.

What flares up quickly burns out quickly.

Most of these overnight successes do not have the experience, or infrastructure, to maintain their momentum long term.

They may have a month, year, or even a few years of success.

But, because they basically fell into success, they will take the rewards as too easy to attain.

They will not respect the rewards.

Such people usually crash and burn financially pretty quickly.

YouTube is full of young Vloggers who throw cash around.

Sure, it gets views and draws in more money.

But the internet is fickle.

They maybe center stage today, and forgot about, or even ridiculed, twelve months from now.

Also, due to their arrogance, they will try ever more audacious stunts to try and replicate their old success.

This is not a business model.

It is a PR stunt.

There is no real infrastructure.

Once the novelty wears off, attention will decline.

Rapidly.

Their whole business model is based on people giving them attention.

No attention equals no revenue.

Hello mediocrity.

Quality content/product + Attention = Revenue.

This is absolutely true.

But, if the product is purely someone throwing money around for attention.

Well, do I need to explain the flaw in this plan?

Keep an eye on some of these young influencers.

They have the shelf life of milk.

Why?

When others see how easy it was to get views and money by doing stupid stuff, then hordes of other, just as qualified people, will try to outdo them.

The saturation of the market by such an influx will make the original person less and less relevant.

Such a market is based on new and shiny.

When it's no longer new and struggles to outshine the hordes of competitors.

It's goodbye attention and therefore revenue.

This is a great example of self-confidence turning into arrogance.

Arrogance backed by a very flimsy, and extremely short-term, business model.

You will see so many of these people fall over the next few years, mark my words.

A young teenager throwing money around and talking about status may be funny now.

But for how long?

How long before they just get boring and irritating?

Just how much will their stunts have to increase in financial expenditure to produce an ever decreasing financial return, just to stay relevant?

I'm sure you get my point.

As I have said, base your confidence in your abilities, not your luck.

If your top venture happens to start to decline, then you will have confidence that you can turn it around or build something new.

If you base your confidence solely on luck and flash in the pan success.

Expect your confidence to decline as fast as your revenue when your luck wears thin and the flash no longer draws attention.

Your self-confidence must be drawn from the loop I described earlier.

The more confidence you have in your abilities, the more you will repeat the actions that produced success.

This positive loop will lead you to success.

You must work on your abilities.

This can only come from taking action.

If you fail, remind yourself that next time you will get better.

Taking action is tied into our next aspect.

Self-Accountability.

You have to hold yourself accountable.

If you fail, it is because you did something wrong, or did not do it well enough.

Do not blame it on luck.

It's a flimsy excuse.

That excuse allows people to alleviate blame from themselves, and to also avoid putting in the hard work to improve their techniques.

Overconfident people do not believe they did the wrong things, they believe they were just "Unlucky."

Newsflash.

If you had done the right things, it would have worked out.

People hate to hear that.

But it's true.

They hate it because it forces them to be self-accountable and admit they didn't perform.

It highlights that they have to improve themselves and their skills or techniques.

The bigger the ego, the more this will impact the individual, and the harder they will resist admitting fault.

This is a complete neglect of self-accountability in action.

Again, you have to be self-accountable.

You do not have a team or employees to blame.

You have your own skills and techniques to hold responsible.

The antidote pill to this hard reality is simple.

Admit to yourself that you need to try harder and improve.

That you were not up to scratch.

The sooner you grasp this concept and apply it, the closer you will move to success.

Why?

Simple.

You will stop and assess what you are doing and look for the faults.

When you find them, you will fix them.

Guess what?

Now you have improved your skills and techniques.

You are better suited to succeed.

This is not rocket science, but how many people do you know that always blame outside factors when they fail?

Yet, when it's a success…Well…Of course that is because they are so great and talented.

See what I mean about the ego aspect?

If that same person refuses to accept and address that they failed by their own doing, how can they re-calibrate for success?

Always be self-accountable.

Be your harshest critic.

Do not fear outside criticism.

Learn the difference between someone being negative for the sake of it and someone who is actually pointing out flaws you may have missed.

If people are negative, then simply drop them out of your life.

You don't need them, and nor should you want them.

However, if someone is giving a valuable critique of your work, then be wise enough to assess what they say.

It may just be the key that unlocks your success.

When receiving critique, always consider the source as closely as the actual criticism.

Today it seems that everyone is entitled to an opinion.

It's true to say that they are entitled to one.

However, too many people go around giving their opinion on matters they know nothing about simply because they feel entitled to have an opinion.

This is a phrase I always say to people when they are feeling down because some character or another gave their uninformed opinion.

"If someone crashed their car every few weeks, would you take driving lessons from them?"

This applies to a significant amount of people these days.

They go around correcting other people and offering solutions when their own life is a mess.

When it comes to finances, it is staggering how many people do this.

You have people who have never been self-employed or done any kind of investing and have yet to do anything significant towards their own financial independence.

They will, however, feel entitled to go around telling people where they are going wrong.

Now don't miss my point here.

If you have someone who is a powerhouse of success, and they are telling you genuine points, then listen closely.

If you have someone who has not practiced what they preach.

Well.

Do I need to tell you?

Your self-accountability also roots deeply into how you manage yourself.

As I said earlier, you do not have anyone behind you pushing you forward.

No manager or boss figure.

No schedule or enforced performance targets.

It's all on you to make sure things get done.

If not, they will not get done.

It will be all your own fault.

Self-accountability.

You should sit down every night and write down your tasks and goals for the next day.

This is not an option.

It is a compulsory part of being your own boss.

Not only will it help you be self-accountable when you check off what you achieved that day.

It will also help you plan your time.

I will go deeper into time management and schedules later in the book.

For now, I will say this much.

It is one hundred percent essential that you sit every night and do the following.

Take a look at the list you wrote the night before and see how many things you checked off.

You then write down what you are going to do tomorrow.

Not attempt or should be able to do.

What you will do.

This list will help you be self-accountable.

If you look at this list at night and realize that you only did a portion, then ask yourself why?

Did that project really need to take three hours?

Or was it because you spent fifty minutes messing on your phone texting a friend and posting on social media about the "Entrepreneur life?"

If you did not complete your day's tasks, be brutally honest with yourself why.

Learn the difference between excuses and reasons.

One can be avoided, and one cannot.

Not completing your tasks because there was a power outage, and therefore no computer, is a reason.

Not completing tasks because you were arguing on social media is an excuse.

If you find that you are making a lot of excuses, then that is a character trait that needs to be fixed.

This can be achieved by self-accountability and self-discipline.

You can see the problem via your accountability.

You can fix it by exercising discipline.

As you have seen so far in this book.

I heavily push reliance on self.

You are your own boss.

You are the one who enforces the schedule, completion of tasks, and attaining of goals on your staff.

You are your staff.

Crazy, but true.

The moment you decided to go it alone, that is exactly what you did.

You became your own boss.

If you were paying another person to perform tasks, turn up on time, and achieve results for your company.

Would you not push them to perform at their best?

So, realize that you are your own boss, and you are your own staff.

You are self-employed, and therefore pay yourself for your results and hard work.

It's a crazy concept, but one that is never mentioned, in my experience at least.

You want to be your own boss.

So be a boss to yourself.

Act like one.
Hold yourself accountable.
Motivate yourself.
Discipline yourself.
Enforce a schedule and task list on yourself.
Expect and demand results from yourself.

Be the boss you need, not the boss you would like.

You need to have the mentality that you need to be a boss that keeps you moving towards success.

If you have the mentality that you want to be a boss that lets you shirk off and covers up for your lackluster performance.

You will fail.

Go get a job and ensure your income.

You are going to fail, and it will be your own fault.

You obviously need someone to push and carry you through life.

You are simply not cut out, nor going to survive in the self-employed world.

Hate those facts?

Then develop and practice self-accountability and discipline.

Without them, you are going to fail.

If you cannot even get out of bed at a reasonable time and enforce a schedule upon yourself.

You are going to fail, and should not risk, becoming self-employed.

If you cannot do a simple self-constructed daily task list, then do not attempt to convince yourself that you are going to set up a successful business, let alone become rich.

It is not going to happen unless by luck.

We discussed that earlier, so if you were paying attention you will know what my standpoint on that is.

You may think I'm being harsh.

I'll tell you what is really harsh.

Lounging around the house for six months and telling everyone you are going to be financially independent from investing and/or starting your own business.

Then having to see those same people and tell them you failed and have had to get a job.

You know the worst part.

The feelings of guilt, regret, and embarrassment knowing that it was all your own fault.

Practice self-accountability to achieve positive results now, rather than practice it later to lament your self-created failures.

The next part we are going to look at is self-discipline and self-motivation.

Again, I ask you to realize this and keep it at the front of your mind.

You are your own boss.

Manage yourself accordingly.

Self-Discipline and Self-Motivation.

The label is on the tin with these concepts.

However, how many people do you know that practice them?

If you want to see it in action, go to your local gym and simply observe the people in the best shape.

They did not get like that by spending the day making excuses as to why laying on the couch is a viable allocation of their time.

They are glowing examples of self-discipline and self-motivation.

In most cases, it is unlikely they have anyone dragging them to the gym and enforcing their diet all day every day.

You could even think of them as bosses of their own health.

They set the schedule, enforce the completion of tasks, and they expect results.

All from themselves.

Do you see the concept I'm trying to put across?

You are the boss of your own financial success.

You cannot avoid having self-discipline and motivation.

They are the wheels on your success vehicle.

You can have the greatest investing plans and business ideas.

It will make no difference if you do not act daily, and consistently, to put them into motion.

This cannot, and will not, happen without self-discipline and motivation.

As I mentioned earlier in the book, your desire fuels your motivation to act and self-discipline keeps you in motion.

These two traits, as with the others I describe, are essential.

Think of building your financial independence like baking a cake.

You have to have all the correct ingredients, in the correct amounts, in order for the cake to turn out as you planned.

Being self-employed is no different.

You cannot be lacking in one department, over-compensate in another, completely ignore another aspect, and expect things to go well.

Self-motivation stems from desire combined with discipline.

If you are not self-motivated, then again, I implore you to either stay at your job or go and get another job.

Self-created financially independent life is not for you.

You have to go to bed excited to get up and work on your ventures.

You have to get up out of bed and plunge straight into your tasks.

As I mentioned, I will talk about schedules later.

I bring this up again because there are aspects, such as maintaining your health and daily errands, that you have to allocate time and focus on.

However, putting that to one side, your main focus and desire should be your ventures.

Your motivation should be so overwhelming that you crave working on them, not dread it.

When you crave something, you will stop at nothing to get it.

When you dread something, you will stop at nothing to avoid it.

Your success has to become an obsession.

It has to be the burning desire that fuels your motivation.

Yes, I have made the point several times.

I'm banging the drum about it, as they say.

Why?

Because it doesn't need to be reinforced, or explained, beyond a superficial level.

If you feel it does, then you should need to question what you claim to desire.

If you want to quit your job, but still struggle to drag yourself out of bed every day.

If you neglect working on your ventures because you just want to lounge on the couch when you get home.

Guess what?

Your desire to succeed is far less than your desire to lay on the couch.

It is that simple and the answer is in your actions.

If you dedicate every spare moment, action, and thought into your ventures, then you are set for success.

Sure, you may stumble and fail along the way.

You may change plans.

But if your desire is great enough, you will be so motivated that you will never quit until you succeed.

Self-discipline is something you must develop to the highest degree possible.

You may already have it, or you may think you are seriously lacking.

In either case, you need to develop it as high as you can on a daily basis.

To assess your personal degree of self-discipline, you need simply look at what you already do.

Do you go to the gym on a consistent basis?

Do you finish any tasks you may start?

Do you get things done when they need doing?

If you go to the gym on a consistent basis, then you already have self-discipline and self-motivation.

You just need to apply that to your business.

If you do not at least exercise on a regular basis, then you are lacking in self-discipline.

Obviously, if someone has conditions that prevent them from doing so, reasons not excuses, then this is a different matter.

But that doesn't excuse you from the other aspects.

If you always complete tasks you start, then again, you hold a degree of self-discipline.

If you constantly start, stop, and abandon tasks, then you may have a self-discipline problem compounded with a focus problem.

If you usually complete errands as they come up, then again, you most likely have at least a basis for self-discipline

The trait is there, it just needs focusing on your business and increasing to higher levels.

If you procrastinate or avoid doing things, then this is an issue that needs to be addressed.

You can learn a lot about your strengths and weaknesses simply by observing your own behavior.

This is why I'm such a big advocate of writing down task lists.

If you consistently complete your lists in a timely and efficient manner, then you most likely have good traits.

If you consistently fail to complete the lists, or are rolling things over to another day repeatedly, then you have to make improvements.

I cannot emphasize enough how important it is to have these traits.

If you disbelieve what I say, then feel free to observe people who have these traits and people who do not.

Their results will prove my point with ease.

The next traits we are going to look at are creativity and adaptability.

If you have the traits discussed so far, self-confidence, self-accountability, self-discipline, and self-motivation.

You will have a firm foundation to reinforce the chances of success for the following traits.

So, let's take a look at creativity and adaptability.

Creative and Adaptable.

You have to be able to think outside of the box, as they say.

The world is constantly evolving, and you have to be able to adapt in order to survive and thrive.

It simply is a fact of life.

For example, entrepreneurs are always looking for systems that produce results.

Of course, we all want that.

True entrepreneurs, however, will create their own systems or adapt an existing one and improve it.

This is the very nature of the entrepreneur.

I think this has got distorted over time to where people think being an entrepreneur is just about being rich.

They forget that successful entrepreneurs are rich because they are entrepreneurs.

There are huge differences between creating a system, adapting one, and merely adopting one.

Everyone seems to be looking for that killer system that just prints money.

Take a step back and look at what they are trying to "adopt" and who has created the system and adapted it to sell in the current market.

Then look at who is rich.

The creator and adapter, or the adopters?

This is why there are so many self-professed internet gurus.

They create or adapt a system, then sell it to people looking to adopt a system.

They become rich, show their success, and now more people want to adopt the system, and the original creator or adapter gets richer.

The adoptees usually have mixed results.

This may be due to the system, or it may be due to the traits of the individual system adoptee.

If they are lacking focus, self-motivation, self-discipline, etc.

This will show in their results regardless of what system they adopt.

Do you see my point now?

You have to have those core traits, and you have to be willing to create and adapt if you are truly committed to becoming successful.

You can adopt whatever system you like, it may be the easiest most profitable system in the world, but there are two key factors.

If you do not have the correct traits and mindset to put in the work to make it successful, it won't be.

If you are not able to be creative and adapt the system as the world changes, then the system will decline in its effectiveness, and so will your income.

You should be able to look at any income system you create or adopt and see either flaws or room for improvement.

Any system.

What is productive today may not be productive at all in five months or in two years.

You should be trying to adapt and evolve your ventures at all times.

As they say, better to be early to a trend than late.

This adaptability and creativity should also apply to yourself.

In fact, it's not a case of should, it is imperative.

You should be constantly looking to improve yourself and adapt to the world around you in order to survive and thrive.

Some people may call this concept "Economic Darwinism."

To be fair, that statement has its merit.

After all, in business, is it not the most adaptable and creative who survive and thrive?

Survival of the fittest?

Businesses that refuse to adapt, and keep evolving, die out all the time.

In economic adversity, such as a crash or severe downturn, the amount of businesses that go under is staggering.

The owners often claim all kinds of external factors such as economic downturn, inflation, deflation, bank rates.

Whatever is deemed an adequate excuse to alleviate the blame from themselves.

My answer is this.

You have businesses that are hundreds of years old and have survived the great depression, world wars, the dot-com bust, 2008, everything.

So, were they just lucky, or was there some kind of secret sauce?

Secret sauce.

They adapted and evolved to the new world forming around them.

Their current economic environment with views to evolve as the future arrived.

That is the secret sauce.

If the owners and top people of the company neglect this fact. Everyone underneath them, employees, suppliers, creditors, can expect to get caught in their spiraling of the drain.

It may not crush them, but they will feel the impact via job losses, lower orders, and defaults.

In easy economic times, it is equally easy for all kinds of people to get a slice of the cake.

In an economic boom, you will see all kinds of people opening businesses.

In a downturn, you will see the majority disappear as quickly as they appeared.

You will also see companies that survive and thrive.

Again, because they adapt and create their way through adversity.

Be willing to proactively learn.

Be willing to try new things and be willing to adapt them.

Be willing to create new systems and adapt them as time goes on.

Again, this stems from self-motivation and the other traits I have mentioned thus far.

You should have a fire to create and the motivation to adapt.

This also stems from self-confidence.

The belief that you are capable and are going to succeed, no matter what happens.

Do you see how it all ties together?

In order for all these things to gel, you need dedication and perseverance.

Things may be hard in the beginning, or get harder as the world evolves.

Rough patches happen for all companies.

It's a test of the company's infrastructure.

If it is built on sand, then it will probably sink.

You are the keystone of your own financial infrastructure and are hopelessly intertwined with it.

If you fail, it fails.

If it fails, you fail.

A group member, can, and in some cases rightly so, blame other members of the group and their actions and decisions.

You, if you are going solo, cannot.

Self-accountability.

If your venture doesn't work, it's because you didn't design and/or implement it correctly.

If your venture fails later, it's because you were not able to create ways to adapt it.

Although it may seem like I'm being harsh, what I am trying to do is encourage you to a position of strength and awareness.

If you develop these traits you stand a far greater chance of success, and sustained success, than anyone who is lacking in what I describe.

You will be the fittest and they will not.

Remember, it is survival of the fittest.

The most adaptable to change.

The strongest innovators.

They survive.

The others.

Well, they end up extinct eventually if they do not adapt to their environment.

They also have to be able to endure the changes as they force them to evolve.

Dedication and Perseverance.

In order to produce success, you have to possess an abundance of dedication and perseverance.

At various stages, the beginning usually, but it can happen at any stage, there will be times when you just have to be patient for results.

You may be tweaking your techniques, system, or product, but simply not getting any results, or not as much as you would like.

Of course, adapt and be creative, but you also have to be dedicated to your plans and willing to persevere through to success.

Too many people expect large results in short time frames.

The truth is, most successful ventures are literally like snowballs.

They start small, and so long as they keep rolling, they will get bigger.

A lot of people expect to push the snowball a couple of times and have a huge ball in front of them.

No, you have to keep pushing and pushing until it reaches the desired size.

It takes motivation, backed with a desire to put in the effort, in order to create the desired snowball.

Crazy example, but it illustrates my point well.

Too many people give up pushing way too early because they have small results and large expectations.

They also lack the motivation and desire to keep pushing.

If you have a great enough desire that motivates you to act, and it is backed by dedicated perseverance and creative adaptability, you will eventually have your snowball.

This is why all these traits tie together.

They feed off and reinforce each other.

If you are dedicated to your goals and persevere, you will eventually have your goals achieved.

Again, if you also creatively adapt, you will survive and thrive in any environment.

This is not to say you should be dedicated and persevere on something that is not working.

You have to have a sense of realism and self-accountability.

As I said, create and innovate your plans into success.

But you have to keep going.

If you abandon your plans too early, then your missing ingredient for success may have simply been the dedication to persevere through adversity.

You need to be obsessed with your success and not willing to ever stop until you achieve it.

Your dedication and perseverance are directly linked to your self-motivation and self-discipline.

Your ability to keep going when others give up.

Become the strongest and combine that with adaptability.

You will then survive and thrive.

It doesn't matter whether you are planning to invest your way to wealth with stocks in this crash, build a business, or any other venture.

You have to be dedicated to your success and persevere till you achieve it.

Resilience and Realism.

You have to be resilient to the knocks and bangs of life, and also realistic with yourself.

It is essential that you are dedicated enough to persevere through adversity, and also be resilient to its up and downs.

However, you also have to be realistic about matters.

You have to be resilient because, as I have mentioned plenty of times, being self-employed is rarely plain sailing.

It may be hard to gain momentum in the beginning, or things may change and impact your business or investments in a negative fashion.

You will have to be resilient in such times.

Resilient enough to see them through and survive the hardships.

You may feel that you are doing everything right, yet nothing seems to be working.

So, persevere through, adapt, and be resilient to the knocks as they come in.

Do not let adversity crush your resilience, because if you do, your self-motivation and all the other traits will be crushed in short order.

Life can be full of success and happiness.

But, rest assured it will be balanced by times that test you.

It's just the nature of the game.

Don't convince yourself that once the crash is out of the way, and things are getting better, that you are immune to problems and can let your guard down.

If you let your guard down and start to lack resilience.

The first major problem may just crush you and your ventures.

If not, then the second, or third, fourth, fifth, may trip you up.

Develop the traits I have described and constantly seek to improve them to greater levels of strength.

Keep adapting to change.

The resilience kicks in during transition.

Change will come.

As they say "Change is the only constant"

Things can, do, and will change.

It's a law of nature, if you will.

You must be adaptable to change as I described.

You also must be resilient while the changes are occurring until you have adapted to a position of strength induced by your traits of perseverance etc.

In the beginning, you must be especially resilient because your new life is just starting.

You are still adapting to being your own boss.

There will be a lot of changes going on in your life.

Without resilience, you will lose the perseverance, and so the rest of the traits will crumble.

You will fail.

Do not let small things go unfixed, but do not let the small things become a bigger impact than they deserve.

This is where being realistic kicks in

You always have to be realistic as to what is happening and why.

You have to enforce this self-awareness upon yourself.

If your venture is not working, take time to look at it and self-analyze as to why.

Be realistic enough to admit problems with yourself and your infrastructure.

Be resilient enough to accept you need improvement, and resilient enough to endure the transitions needed.

Do not ever kid yourself away from realism, with yourself, or your ventures.

For example, if you are investing in a stock and the company is looking like it is in trouble, do not let any amount of hashtag hype influence your investing decisions.

If you are building a business and it's not working, be realistic as to why.

Time And Money Management

When self-employed, time and money management are imperative.

Time Management.

When you are self-employed, you are the master of your own time.

Well, at least that's how it appears on the surface.

You work for yourself and get to set your own schedule.

It's cool to tell friends how you are free to do what you want all day while they complain about job schedules, and not being able to get time off for vacations when they want to.

However, you can expect to have your time allocated out even more ruthlessly.

By yourself.

It's a known fact that some of the world's most famous entrepreneurs work eighteen hours a day, seven days a week.

That's 126 hours a week.

Yes, more than three times the amount of the average person's job obligations.

Think back to desire, motivation, self-discipline etc.

Do you think they are lacking any of the traits I described, or do you think they are core to their success?

Such entrepreneurs may be running huge companies or networks of companies.

Thousands of people depending on them to make the company successful so that the employees remain in a job.

Do you think there's a degree of self-confidence and self-accountability at play in these entrepreneurs?

It's a sure bet that there's a fair degree of self-motivation involved.

Dedication and perseverance?

I think I've made my point.

One of the skills these people also have is time management.

Granted, they most likely have personal assistants and secretaries filling in their schedule with appointments, etc.

But the fact remains, they are paying someone to manage their time.

That is how important time management is.

As your own boss, you have to do this for yourself.

It also has to be backed by self-discipline, and self-accountability.

You should look at your plans and of course assign tasks to each of the steps.

I do this, then this, then that, and that aspect is in place.

You need to then allocate time frames to complete these steps.

An over-arching timeframe and an individual task time frame spread.

To clarify:

The overarching timeframe might be, you want a website up and running in two weeks.

The task timeframe may look something like this:

Set up basics such as domain, web platform, social media accounts, opt-in software.

So now you would look at the likely timeframe of each task.

Research and set up domain: 30 minutes.

Set up web platform: 30 minutes.

Claim Social media accounts: 1 hour.

Set up opt-in software basics: 30 minutes.

Then you would set up tasks such as, fill out website infrastructure and base content, fill out basic social media templates, set up opt-in welcome emails.

So, your next set of tasks may look like this:

Website infrastructure and base content: 5 hours.

Social Media Templates: 3 hours.

Set up opt-in email welcome emails: 1 hour.

This all adds up to 11.5 hours at this point.

A dedicated and organized person with time management skills backed with solid traits can do this in one day.

Do you realize how long it takes some people?

Take a guess.

Weeks, even months, if at all.

I'm not joking.

Having a long list of tasks can seem overwhelming, but not if you allocate reasonable time frames to them.

You can literally achieve in a matter of days what most people take weeks or months to achieve.

Again, I ask, who is the most likely to be successful, and in the shortest time frame?

The skill of time management alone will put you vastly ahead of most people.

Rest assured, they may be talking a big game, but they are most likely not taking much in the way of action.

When the truth comes out in the form of actual results, not the touting of distant future goals, you will obliterate them.

This may sound harsh or aggressive, but as I said, this is survival of the fittest.

Do you think they will be tossing and turning at night worrying about you if they have achieved their goals of mansions and Ferraris, and you have not?

It's not about being hostile, just competitive.

If you want to win a race, then you simply run faster than everyone else in the race.

To do that you have to train harder than your competitors so that when the time comes, you are the stronger runner.

Business is no different.

If you wish to be successful, then you have to be better than the competitors in your market.

This is done by training and working hard.

Yes of course there is always the work smarter aspect.

But that again reinforces the creative and adaptability traits from earlier.

The fact of the matter is, whoever works the hardest, and most effectively, will win the business game.

I don't care what business you are in, there are x amount of dollars spent in that business every year.

This is why you hear talk of market share by big businesses.

Despite growth and fluctuations, every year there are X amount of dollars spent.

Could be more this year, and less next year.

But there will be a total amount for the year.

Big businesses aim to capture as many of those dollars as they can.

When you are self-employed, you need to work hard and smart.

Smart involves utilizing your time effectively.

Thus, time management is a skill you need to keep on point.

When you have set your tasks and allocated time frames, you need to prioritize.

If you know that tasks A and D are dependent on task A being completed, then of course you should work on that first and aim to complete it in a timely manner.

Sounds obvious right?

It's amazing how many people will jump from task to task because they get bored or prefer working on another.

Half-finished or rarely posted to websites enter stage left.

What could have taken maybe a few hours to set up, and two hours a day to maintain in order to achieve results, has been pushed aside for weeks.

Simply because they are getting likes on their social media pictures.

An effective person would have had it all set up within a day or two and would be working on social media to drive traffic to their website and creating revenue.

If you are investing and not setting up any kind of business venture, then you should still account for your time.

Allocate time to study what is going on in the markets and to keep an eye on both current and future investments.

Just because you are an investor it doesn't mean you can ignore time management.

Treat your investing like a business.

Make sure you are sitting at your computer when the market opens.

Many investors have been caught out by not keeping track of what is going on, not only in the wider market, but also in the sectors they are invested in.

Some news has been released overnight and individual stocks have either surged or tanked in price, all while the investor was rotting in bed.

As an investor, allocate your time to investing ventures.

If nothing is actually going on in the market, then use the time to research future moves and opportunities.

Money Management.

You are going to need to be good at managing your money.

I don't care whether that's at the early stages when you are on a shoestring budget, or later when you have money to burn.

At both stages, lack of money management will lead to problems, if not disaster.

If you do not manage it correctly in the early stages, you will run out of the money your business or investing ventures need to survive and thrive.

If you somehow manage to bungle your way through to success, and still lack money management skills when money is in abundance, then do not expect it to last long term..

Many are the tales of famous celebrities who made staggering fortunes in a short space of time and who ended up flat broke.

This is purely due to poor money management.

Easy come, easy go, as they say.

That applies to everyone with poor money management skills.

You have to make sure every penny is accounted for and spent wisely for maximum effect and return if possible.

If you have quit your job, or lost your job due to the crash, yet still spend like you have an employed income, then problems will arise.

You cannot spend more than you need to before you have income.

Results from your venture.

You may project that you will be earning $10k a month within three months, but you don't KNOW for certain that this will be the case.

You simply don't.

You can believe it, but you don't know it as a certain fact.

This said, you should live way below your means as much as possible in the beginning.

I'm not saying starve yourself, wear rags, and become a hermit.

Though this may become the case if you blow through your money too early.

As I said earlier, it's best to test the water before you quit your job and try out your plans to see if they work at a base level.

You may then deduce that you should allocate more time, quit your job, and scale those results to greater heights.

But, unless you have a significant cash reserve, as close to a year as you can get, plus business money, plus extra backup investments, then you should be very wary of quitting your job.

When I took the jump, I had a significant cash reserve, plus assets, plus my business infrastructure was already paid for.

I was just lacking time and wanted to be free from the distractions that come with the job I had.

The revenue declining at the job was my tipping point, but that was just the push I needed.

I was already standing on the edge ready to jump anyway.

I will admit, the first month or two, I spent like I always had when money was flowing in.

But this was because I could, and the money was not wasted, it was spent fairly wisely.

After a while I slowed down, knowing that if I did, I would have more guaranteed time to work on my business.

My earnings were not guaranteed, but the money I had around me was enough so long as I didn't waste it in a short time frame through poor money management.

As I said, I lived below my means, still better than most to be honest, but not enough to steer me into trouble.

You should aim to do the same.

When you are self-employed and no one managing your time for you, it is very easy to fill that time with things you like that also drain your money.

You should judge every purchase as an asset or a liability.

It will either produce more money, or take it away never to return from whence it went.

Obviously, food and bills are essential liabilities.

Clothes you need, but, going out blowing money on expensive clothes so you can embellish your entrepreneur dress-up game is a liability and foolish.

People say dress for success.

I say dress to your status and not your aspired status.

Sure, if your business model involves meeting people and you need to put on a good appearance, then that is wise spending.

Your investment in clothes is an asset of sorts because it may land you deals that bring in revenue.

Dressing to impress your friends or for likes on your social media entrepreneur masquerade page is a liability.

Again, I'm not saying dress like you are broke if you are not and don't want to.

I am, however, saying don't let the spending outpace returns or needs.

When buying things for your business; use the same mindset.

Is this for vanity or revenue?

Am I paying a big amount for a website template when I could just get a free one and spend time upgrading it manually?

If you decide to buy a new computer. Is that because you are trying to be more efficient for your business, or just because it's a treat to yourself?

As I have stated, if your income from your ventures allow this, and it is beneficial, then sure, buy it.

If you are not earning anything and your current computer will do the job for now, then be shrewd and exercise self-discipline in your spending.

Self-accountability also plays into this of course.

Time, spending, everything.

Do not start the habit of making self-justifications for bad decisions based on desire.

Self-justify why you *shouldn't* spend more often than self-justify why you *should*.

If the self-justification of why you *should* significantly and realistically outweighs the justification of not spending, then fine, go ahead.

But if your only self-justification is "It's cool and I want it." Well, you are in bad habit territory and a slippery slope.

The Internet

A topic I have mentioned repeatedly in this book is the internet and online skills.

As I have said, many businesses, regardless of future lockdowns or not, have learned their lesson with regards to having an online presence.

At least I hope so!

Time will tell.

Many are going to be looking for people with the skillsets needed to operate online and also possibly work remotely.

So even if you are not interested in building up assets or your own online business, then you should still aim to develop your online skillset.

If your current job falls through, or if you have already been laid off, (I wish you all the best and hope you get a new income or job soon) then you will still be able to take advantage of the coming online goldrush.

I call it this, simply because the amount of online revenue is set to increase dramatically in my opinion.

I am not alone in this belief.

Many people, including economic experts, are saying similar things.

I have already covered the aspects of people moving to online shopping before the outbreak, and the surge during the lockdown.

But it is worth noting the following point.

The online revenue models were experiencing serious growth before the outbreak and lockdown.

While other business models collapsed in revenue due to the lockdown, the online models surged even more.

Pretty simple concept to grasp.

When other businesses were operating as normal, the online businesses surged.

When the offline models collapsed, the online models surged even more.

It really is that simple.

Sooner or later, more and more people are going to figure that out.

They may not be too late to the party, but they will still be later than those who acted sooner.

My advice is to learn the skills needed to operate online.

You most likely have a basic grasp of social media, so aim to build upon that knowledge and either produce your own revenue or at least have skill sets that employers will be looking for.

The online skill sets are pretty varied and numerous.

You do not have to learn them all.

After all, a jack of all trades is a master of none.

But that does not mean that you do not need to be at least aware of the core sets.

If you are looking at developing skills for employment, then you should look at things such as social media and online marketing in general.

If you are looking at building your own income streams, then you should look at aspects such as, social media and online marketing, but also SEO (Search Engine Optimization) and perhaps website building.

Website building is nowhere near as hard as it used to be.

In the past, it involved all kinds of coding and back-end wizardry.

These days, there are many "Drag and drop" software platforms that allow you to build a website base within minutes.

You can then modify the templates by literally dragging and dropping elements to make the site look and function as you wish.

There are even plenty of free options online for you to try.

Some platforms still require a learning curve, but some are so simple that children are able to set up sites within minutes.

You could also perhaps learn how to edit videos and look into that aspect of the online skillset.

Again, there is software available that is easy to learn and use, and there is software that has a learning curve.

There is no need to try to run before you can walk.

Take it steady and progress at your own pace.

Lots of people across the globe are currently sitting locked up in their homes all day.

Businesses are closed and people are mostly online.

Watching movies and shows.

Trawling social media.

Shopping online.

The world is literally a captive audience at this point.

Do you know who is making a lot of money while others are sitting around spending and worrying?

Online entrepreneurs.

Can you imagine how many views YouTube channels are getting now people are sitting at home all day?

Just how much money are Affiliate Marketers making posting links to products on social media at this time?

I could go on and on.

Last December, offline retail sales were not pretty for the holiday season, but online sales soared.

Feel free to look into that and see what I mean.

With the current situation, and the problems that are most likely coming in my opinion, a lot of people are going to be looking for ways to make money.

If you do not learn online skills at this point, you are quite frankly in my opinion, missing an amazing opportunity.

People are increasingly moving their shopping to online venues.

If the economic situation goes the way I predict, and the signs are there, then crime is going to uptick sharply.

As people lose their jobs and the economy starts to suffer, street crime will increase notably, in my opinion.

This will lead to even more people shopping online.

As businesses get less foot traffic in malls etc, then they will increase their online presence.

Considering people can, and often do, order things online via a couple of taps on their phone these days.

People with online skills are going to make a fortune in the coming years.

There are no two ways about it.

So, let's take a look at how to set up your very own online business.

How To Set Up An Online Business

In this course, you will learn the basics of setting up an online work-from-home business.

Many "Internet Gurus" will charge you a lot of money for a pre-packaged course with similar information.

Others will even charge you a monthly membership fee to a site that holds this basic information.

Simply follow through the steps and you will learn the basics of online marketing.

Their courses may be fluffed out and have pitches for "Secret" techniques in order to make them appear worth their price tag.

The truth of the matter is, you will have to learn the basics before you can even hope to understand the advanced techniques.

Most of these "Secret" techniques are often just spins on the basics that use SEO loopholes and are often obsolete within short periods of time.

Once you have the basics of this course completed and understood, THEN, you can consider advanced techniques.

Although at first glance setting up an online business seems to be a daunting prospect, the concept is actually quite straightforward.

On the surface it appears full of terminology and "Tech speak"

I'm going to break some of this down for you.

I'm sure that if you are reading this, you have seen all the self-proclaimed gurus touting their courses that will make you a millionaire in six months.

Let me tell you this straight off the bat.

They make THEIR millions from selling YOU their courses.

I'm not saying that their courses do not work.

What I am saying is that what they are selling is decorated basics.

Regardless of what techniques they stick on the outside, the core aspects are usually the same.

So, without further delay, let's proceed to step 1.

Step 1 – What are you going to do?

Your first decision is, what are you going to do?

There are many ways of making money online.

All have their own nuances, but all will use at least some, if not all, of the basics I'm going to teach you here.

First, you have to decide what kind of products you are going to be promoting online.

I'm going to break down the most common to give you some ideas.

Own products.

The most obvious route to take is to sell your own products.

This can be basically anything these days.

There are plenty of manufacturers that will create and label items for you.

There are also lots of platforms that will handle sales transactions and even shipping for you.

You may already have some ideas on what you want to do, but here are some common ones.

Physical items.

There are companies today that will create, label, and even package, pretty much any product you can think of.

If, for example, you wished to start a fitness supplement brand, there are companies online that offer the following business model.

You create a brand name and logo.

Be sure to look into any relevant licensing and other aspects relevant to the particular business and products you choose to do.

You then find a company that produces the products you are aiming to create and sell.

This can be done with simple Google searches such as "Custom protein powder manufacturers" for example.

They will then have built-in software on their website that will allow you to create your own mix of ingredients.

A pre-workout supplement may be, x amount of caffeine, x amount of this, etc.

Once you are satisfied with your blend, you would then be presented with a price on single units, bulk units, etc.

Next, you would upload your logo and design your packaging.

Once you are happy with that, you would then go to the checkout cart and place your order.

The product would be manufactured and shipped to your address and you now have your own physical product line ready to sell.

You could then either set up an online store with a platform such as Shopify to sell and ship the products yourself.

Or set up an Amazon account, send the products to their distribution center, and they handle all the shipping to the customers.

That is a very basic overview to give you an idea of how creating an online physical product business works.

I have not gone into things such as licensing, setting up accounts with the manufacturer, banks, shopping platforms, etc.

Each individual business and product will have its own procedures that are far beyond the scope of this guide. So be sure to do your own research before committing to any ventures.

It is purely an example of a basic structure.

Pretty much any kind of physical product you can think of can be handled the same way these days.

Clothing companies that will stitch your logo on base units or even manufacture custom products that you design from scratch.

Glassware that can be etched with logos or designs.

Custom board games that can have everything from the board, pieces, packaging, everything, manufactured according to the designs you upload.

Jewelry and watches designed to your specifications.

Physical copies of books that you have written. (Known as print on demand)

Almost anything you can think of can now be custom designed and manufactured for you on the internet.

As I said, you can set up a shopping cart software such as Shopify and sell to your customers online from there.

The payments and shipping details will be handled through the software and you can ship the products to the customers yourself.

Amazon offers a service (FBA, Fulfilled by Amazon) that allows you to sell directly from their platform.

It includes software that allows you to create listings just the same as any other product on Amazon.

You can send your products to the Amazon distribution center and they will handle shipping, customer service, etc.

Digital products.

You can also create your own digital products that can be sold online and downloaded by your customers.

No need for physical inventory manufacturing, storage, or shipping.

This is my personal favorite Lone Wolf Entrepreneur business model.

Unlimited inventory and instantaneous delivery.

I will give you a process example, and then some examples of digital products you can create.

Example

You have written a book in software such as Microsoft Word.

You can then go and join a platform such as Amazon KDP (Kindle Distribution Platform)

You would then upload your book file and format it for Kindle using the software on the platform.

Next, you would upload, or use the software to create, your book cover.

Then you would fill in all the other details, such as book description and pricing, for the listing on Amazon.

Once approved it will be available for sale on Amazon just like any other product.

When a customer purchases the digital book, Amazon will handle the payment and the customer will download the book straight to their electronic device within a few seconds.

You then get credited with your profit (Royalty) and paid straight to your bank account on the next pay date.

As you can see, that is a great business model!

What is also great, is that if you sell a lot of copies in a short period of time, you will rise in the sales rankings and therefore be exposed to even more potential customers.

Considering the traffic and global reach of Amazon, this can be extremely lucrative.

There are many other digital products you can create and sell online.

Here are some examples.

Apps can be created by yourself using online creation platforms or by outsourcing the work to people with coding skills.

Photographs can be taken and uploaded to platforms such as BigStock. When people download the pictures for use on blogs, or other online ventures, they pay a fee, and you get a royalty each time.

Visual comics can be created using online platforms and they can then be uploaded to platforms for sale by download.

Digital artwork can be created and then sold for use as book covers or interior artwork for projects.

Indie video games created by sole developers or small teams can be uploaded to platforms such as Steam for sale by download. There are software platforms that allow people to create games with a small budget and limited coding experience.

There are many other kinds of digital products you can create and sell online.

Third-party products.

Another thing you can sell online is other people's products.

This can be done in several ways.

Purchase products at wholesale prices and simply add your profit into the price that you actually sell it for to the customer.

Straight forward business model.

Simply look online for wholesalers of your chosen product type, then set up a Shopify or Amazon as described above.

You can also do what is known as "Drop-shipping"

Drop-shipping is almost the exact same business model, except instead of handling all the shipping yourself, or joining the Fulfilled by Amazon program, it is done slightly differently.

With drop shipping, you would select products and add a profit to the final price as per the previous business model

You would then create listings for customers to view, select, and purchase products, same as before.

The difference is, when you sell an item, you take the money from the customer, get their shipping details, and then contact the wholesaler.

You would then pay the wholesaler the cost price, any shipping charges, and they would send the product straight to the customer.

The profit you added is yours to keep, and you don't have to physically handle the products for shipping or keep an inventory of your own.

You can list anything the manufacturer sells and simply follow the process above.

You can google "Dropshipping companies" for more details.

Yet another way is to do what is known as affiliate marketing.

This concept is actually extremely simple.

A lot of companies have what are known as affiliate programs.

These programs pay people a referral fee if they refer any customers who make a purchase.

For example.

Jim joins the Amazon affiliate program.

He is given access to software tools that allow him to create a link that will direct anyone who clicks on it to the product page on Amazon.

The link also contains a special I.D. that is Jim's own unique affiliate I.D.

Jim posts the links on his social media and blog as product recommendations.

When a person reads his social media or blog post, they will see the product recommendations and perhaps click the link.

They will then be taken to the product page on Amazon.

If they purchase the product, it will all be handled by Amazon as usual.

The price and process are absolutely no different than if they purchased the product without clicking on the affiliate link.

The difference is, Amazon will pay Jim a percentage of the sale as a referral fee.

Think of it like Jim being an online salesperson.

If he promotes a product and someone buys it from the third party, they pay him a commission.

Many of the largest online shopping sites have affiliate programs.

For example, Google "Amazon affiliate program" and you will see information on Amazon's program.

They will pay you a percentage for referrals on almost any product that can be found on their site.

Many sites have affiliate programs, so simply visit a company you may have in mind and check their site for details or Google them the same way as I suggested with Amazon's affiliate program.

For the rest of this section, I'm going to assume that you have chosen what kind of products you are going to be selling and focus on the actual infrastructure and promotional aspects.

If you have not yet decided what kind of products or business you want to do, don't worry!

You can always read through this section and then decide what you want to do later.

This is simply the basic aspects of setting up an online business.

*Take note that business licensing and other aspects are not included in this course. That is something you will have to research for yourself with regards to your chosen business field.

Step 2 – Choose a name and research domains and social media.

The first thing you need to do is to choose a name for your business.

The reason this is very important as the first step is that you will need to check domain name and social media name availability if you are going to be selling online.

You may decide that you are going to start a company called "Jim's discount gaming laptops"

Nothing wrong with that, but, what if the domain name and/or social media name are already taken?

So, let me first explain what a domain name is.

A domain name is the web address, URL, of your website.

(URL stands for Universal Redirection Link)

So, the business name may be "Jim's discount gaming laptops"

The domain name should ideally be *jimsdiscountgaminglaptops.com*

He would also want his social media account names to be the same or as similar as the platforms allow.

Some social media platforms only allow a certain number of characters for account names.

Jim may have to use the name "Jim's gaming laptops" on some platforms, for example.

How to research these aspects is actually very easy.

To research the domain of your choice, simply go to a domain registrar such as Godaddy.com

Type in the domain name of your business and see if it is available.

Godaddy, or any other registrar, will show you the price and availability of the domain and any similar variations.

If your choice is already gone, then you will have to either get a domain as close to it as you see fit, or think of another business name.

I'm assuming for the purpose of this course that you have not yet set up your business officially with licenses etc.

As you can see, the step of researching your domain is very important.

If you go out and set up your business before researching your domain, you may find that the domain is already gone.

My advice on domain names, besides matching your business name, is to make them memorable.

Do not pick anything that is too bizarre or with bizarre spellings.

The reason is that sometimes people may recommend your site by word of mouth or simply type up the name to share on social media rather than post an actual link.

If the name is not easy to remember or spell, then it can lead to lost business.

Choose whatever business name and domain you wish, but, bear that fact in mind.

The same logic also applies to social media.

If your name is hard to remember, it can lead to similar issues.

To research your social media accounts, simply go to the platforms you wish to be present on and search to see if the names are available.

With some platforms, you may have to join before being able to search.

If need be, set up an email account with a service such as Gmail, then join the social media platform to see if you can set up an account using your desired business name.

Before settling on a business name, you should also do a Google search to see what, if any, domains are ranking in search results for that name.

You may find sites and businesses with names very similar, or you may find that it just gives information related to the words you type in.

Jim may find a lot of information on laptops, but no similar domains in results, for example.

The reason for this is that the word "Laptops" is what is known as a keyword.

A keyword is something related to certain information.

So, if jimsdiscountgaminglaptops.com is not taken, searching for it may bring up sites related to the search.

Gaminglaptops.com and discountgaminglaptops.com may appear in Google search results, for example.

We will get deeper into keywords later in the course.

Once you have researched the availability of your domains and social media, you should then research what kind of platform you are going to use.

Step 3 – Choosing a platform.

Your platform is the software you are going to use to create your website.

You may for example choose to use a site such as Shopify.

This platform is aimed at people who wish to sell directly from their site.

For example, if you opened a novelty candle business, you may wish to use that software and have your ability to handle payments built-in.

On the other hand, you could decide to use the Fulfilled by Amazon platform and list your products directly on Amazon.

They would handle the payment aspects for you within their platform.

This is something you will have to decide for yourself and what is best for your business model.

If you choose to do something like affiliate marketing, then you would need a blogging platform.

A blogging platform allows you to create articles that appear in Google search results.

This can also be great for your business because you may find customers for your products without them having to search for your site directly.

For example, you may have your fitness supplement business primarily running on Amazon.

You may write a lot of articles related to fitness on your blog and include links to your Amazon product pages.

If people find your articles in Google search results and read them, they may end up clicking on your links and buying your products from your Amazon pages.

This is a kind of marketing I will get to further on in the course.

Authors who sell their books on other platforms can also benefit from having a blog.

The concept is the same.

You may write posts to tell people about upcoming releases or perhaps character backstories not found in your books.

Again, if these posts turn up in Google results, or are shared on social media, it may drive people to your product pages.

There are so many platforms available today that to cover them all is simply unfeasible.

A simple Google search for "Website builders" will bring up plenty of results.

I will give you some background knowledge, so you are more informed in your choice.

A lot of platforms will offer free options and also paid options.

Typically, the free options will not allow you to use your own domain name.

For example, let's say there is a service called freeblog.com.

If Jim uses their free option, his domain would be freeblog.com/jimsdiscountgaminglaptops

I personally advise against using this option.

It looks unprofessional for your business, is usually bad for search engine rankings, and is not exactly memorable.

If you are setting up a professional online business, then at least have a professional domain name.

It will serve you far better.

You may also encounter the terms "WYSIWYG" or "Drag and Drop"

This refers to the type of way you can build the site.

Most business owners do not know any coding or have any website building experience.

The above types of software make building a website very easy, even for complete beginners.

"WYSIWYG" stands for "What You See Is What You Get"

Basically, if you drag an element such as a picture and drop it on to the website design page.

It will appear on the website when it is online exactly as you see it while you are on the design page.

If you change the size of the picture, or add a caption underneath, same thing.

Drag and Drop is simply another name for this concept.

This may seem obvious to you, but, some software platforms require you write code to make things happen.

You may add a picture, but, in order to move it over the page, you may have to change parameters in the coding of the template.

My advice to you on choice of platform is to do your research online and see which is the best fit for your business, design ideas, ability, and also budget.

Most platforms are beginner-friendly, competitively priced, have great customer support and tutorials, and also a wide variety of features such as integrated shopping cart software.

Do some online research and read multiple reviews for any that interest you.

Do not settle with one good review, they may be promoting the platform for commission.

View multiple reviews and cross-reference the information.

Just be sure to choose a platform that has what you need according to your business model.

If you plan to sell directly from your site, then ensure it has reliable and well-rated shopping cart integration.

If you plan on blogging as well, be sure that is an option or feature.

As I said above, I personally advise having blogging as part of your promotional campaign, regardless of what you are selling.

Granted, it doesn't suit every single business model, but most benefit from it.

I mentioned fitness articles and author blog posts above.

But here is another random example to illustrate my point.

Let's say you have a novelty candle business that is using Amazon as its selling platform.

The business could still have a blog and create posts that may draw interest to the products.

Posts could be written about how the candles are made, announce new lines, or anything else that potential customers may find interesting.

These posts would contain pictures and links to the products on the Amazon sales pages.

The posts would not only be visible to anyone who visits the blog homepage (Main page), but they could also turn up in Google search results for people searching for "How candles are made" etc.

These posts can also be shared on social media to the account followers.

If they in turn share them, the posts may get many views and therefore reach potential customers.

It's a very useful way to market your products, but again, research platforms according to your needs and aims.

Step 4 – Choosing social media platforms.

I mentioned researching social media platforms in Step 1 with relation to your domain and social media account names research.

However, here I'm going to go into further detail.

There are many social media platforms available today.

Some are household names with huge user bases, and some are obscure with humble numbers of users.

But, just because one is huge and well known, it does not mean it is the best option for your business model.

Some platforms are almost solely visual-based, and others allow for bodies of text with links.

For example, Instagram is all about pictures, but allows for very little text and no links, apart from one in the account bio.

You may be able to post great pictures of your candles, but you cannot link to the sales page for each product in the picture.

You would have to tell people in the post that there is a link to your website in your bio.

Pinterest will allow you to post a picture, write a description, and add a link to a page each time, as well as allowing you to link your homepage in your bio.

Facebook will allow a similar setup.

This is not to say Instagram is bad in any way.

It has a HUGE user base and can be very effective, but it has its own rules and best practices for success.

As always, you need to research which ones are best for your needs and aims.

YouTube is a fantastic social media promotion platform.

You can create video content, post links in the descriptions, and interact with potential customers in the comments section.

It certainly should not be ruled out of your social media platform choices without some careful consideration.

The results that can be gained from YouTube could be amazing for your business, plus it allows people to subscribe so you can build a follower/customer list.

Twitter will also allow you to post pictures, a small amount of text (280 characters) and a link to your sales pages.

At the moment, the ones I have mentioned are pretty much all of the "Top dogs" as far as social media.

This does not mean you should not look into other options.

It also does not mean you should be present on all of them.

Social media can be time-consuming.

Once your follower base grows, you will start getting questions, comments, and direct messages, etc.

It is always good practice to answer as many of these as possible, and as in a timely manner as possible.

Someone may be one question away from making a purchase, or may really appreciate your help and share your post as a sign of gratitude.

If you consistently ignore comments and questions, people will think you don't care.

That is not good for business.

Customer care is a huge deal for large companies, there's good reason for that.

Someone who has a good experience with your company and products may tell a few people.

Someone who has a bad experience will tell anyone that will listen.

In the age of viral social media posts, you are wise to avoid needless negative experiences.

Besides, you should value your customers, current or potential.

They are the lifeblood of your business.

Treat them as important, because they are.

Without customers, you simply have a selection of products.

Customers bring the money, which is what business is all about.

That said, if you are present on too many platforms, you could find yourself spending a great deal of time on social media instead of working on other aspects of your business that may need attention.

You do not want to spread yourself too thin.

Remember, the point of this book is to set up a Lone Wolf Entrepreneur work from home business.

Do not try to do a team's load of work on your own.

Pick and optimize your social media carefully.

I would suggest, two, maybe three, platforms at most.

You can choose only one if that's what you see fit, but there is no point in missing out on revenue opportunities if you don't have to.

Again, each platform takes a different approach and demands a different workload.

Taking a picture and posting it on Instagram is not time-consuming.

Writing a post on Facebook is no great hardship, but not as simple as just taking a picture.

Creating a video, editing it, and uploading it to YouTube, is a whole different beast.

So, choose your platforms carefully and take into consideration not only potential reach and revenue, but also the time and attention needed.

Something else to consider is whether your potential customer base is present in substantial numbers on the platform.

Most types of customers can be found on most platforms.

However, times change, and so do trends.

Instagram has a broad user base, but you are actually more likely to find a younger demographic on there, rather than the one found on Facebook.

This is not to say young people do not use Facebook.

But, it is becoming increasingly common to hear younger people say "No one uses Facebook these days"

Doubt me?

Look into it online.

I'm not for one second saying Facebook is dead, dying, or should not be part of your marketing.

I'm saying trends occur, and Instagram is where the younger demographic spends most of their time, whether they have Facebook or not.

A way to discern if your target customer base is on a platform is simply to search hashtags and groups.

For example, if I research a platform for entrepreneurs, I simply enter #entrepreneurs or search for "Entrepreneur groups" etc.

If I see a lot of current posts with lots of interaction, then I know that it has a thriving entrepreneur user base.

Same goes for groups, if there are lots of groups, and some groups with large follower bases, I know it's a suitable place.

If posts are old, or have very limited interaction via comments and shares, then it may not be the place I'm looking for.

Apply the same principles to your business.

Think of things you would search for related to your business and take a look around the platform.

See if it's worth your business having an account on the platform.

Remember, being on social media takes time out of your day.

Time spent on a pointless account just to stay current can be spent on an account that provides results.

With most social media, it is a case of attracting followers by creating content that people enjoy.

If you post good quality content, then people will follow you and also share your content with others, and that, in turn, helps you attract more followers and so the cycle goes.

Each platform has its own nuances and techniques, but the core concept is always the same.

Create content that causes people to follow you and share your content with others.

Step 5 – Email marketing.

Some people will say email marketing is dead, a dinosaur that went extinct when social media arrived.

I advise not to be so quick to dismiss it.

Granted, it is not the powerful tool that it once was.

Spammers saw to that.

But, most of those same spammers have now moved to social media.

I mentioned earlier in the book about this and how people abuse comments and direct messages on social media.

I touched upon that and email marketing in the "Following" section of this book.

I won't heavily cover old ground again, but I will state the case for having an email opt-in form on your website.

I will tell you why I think you should, and why I sometimes don't on my ventures.

Why you should.

An email list is YOUR list.

A social media account can be closed at a moment's notice.

It is not unheard of for accounts to be closed over the smallest of matters.

When it is closed, the follower list is gone.

You can't get access to it.

Now, this is not to say it just happens randomly without cause and can't be appealed.

But I have known accounts to be closed much to the shock of their owners, who then scramble to appeal.

Almost always, they get them back.

But not always.

Social media platform terms of service can be very fickle and change with the wind.

One day they may allow affiliate links, and the next they close a whole swathe of accounts because some people have been abusing the platform with affiliate link spam.

Now, you may be thinking, well, I'm not going to do affiliate marketing.

No, but did you know some platforms used to allow links to products and then banned them due to spamming, etc?

Imagine if you have built your entire business around that platform and then overnight it's a banned practice?

Imagine if what you were doing on Tuesday, can get your account locked on Wednesday?

It happens.

Not often, and can usually be appealed.

But there are plenty of people sharing their stories online about how they had their account locked overnight and their appeals have been denied.

Feel free to do some Google research on the matter.

With an email list, it's yours.

It can't be taken away or locked with terms of service changes.

Granted, if you abuse Spam laws, then that's a different tale.

But, an honest business owner that acts responsibly has nothing to fear.

Email lists allow you to market directly to people who WANT to hear from you.

In order to be on the list, they have to "Opt-in"

In other words, they have to agree to you sending them emails by filling out a form on your site, and also agreeing again when the confirmation email turns up in their inbox.

Social media is a constant stream of posts.

It can be very hard to stand out because that is exactly what everyone else is trying to do.

Get noticed.

Email is direct to the people on your list.

Below, in the promotional section, I will tell you how to utilize this tool effectively.

Why I don't always use Email lists.

To be quite honest, I should use them more.

It is simply a case of time.

I work on various ventures and projects every single day.

I mentioned earlier about how I trimmed down what I was doing to achieve results.

Quite frankly, I can't justify the time needed to create newsletters at this point.

It really is a matter of time for me.

I have methods that provide results for me, and I try to focus my time on those.

Why wouldn't I?

Also, I don't usually have an array of products to offer.

Usually one or two, at most, per venture.

So, it is not usually worth creating a regular newsletter to talk about the same things every time.

I'm sure from a subscriber's point of view, they don't want to hear the same things each time either.

If you have a business with a changing line of products, then I advise an email list.

It can be a great marketing tool to promote new releases, but, if like me, you tend to have one or two fixed products...

You can risk coming across as a constant sales pitch.

It all depends on your business model, as I will describe in the promotion step.

How to choose an email marketing software.

There are many great email marketing platforms.

The three most well-known are, Aweber, Get Response, and Mailchimp.

I'm not promoting any of these options, or pushing one over another.

I'm simply making you aware of their existence.

Each has its pros, cons, features, and pricing plans, so you will have to research which one you think is best for you.

Each one works on the same premise.

You would join and set up your account etc.

They will then allow you to create an email list and an opt-in form for that list.

The form can then be added to your website.

Again, on some website builders, this will be very easy, and on others, it may require just a little extra work.

But the concept is the same.

The opt-in form is on your site ready for people to fill in and join your list if they so wish.

You can then create simple emails or newsletters to send to your list.

When created, you push send, and everyone on that list gets the same email or newsletter.

That is the basic concept.

The ability to email large amounts of customers in one go.

The companies are fully compliant with spam laws and often have agreements to be on a "white list" with email services such as Gmail so your emails do not end up in spam folders.

Your newsletters will go straight to their inbox ready to be viewed.

Step 6 – The basics of content creation.

In this step, we will look at the basics of laying out your site and what kind of content you should have there.

Layout.

When you create your site, you will most likely be using a template from the platform you chose.

Most platforms have hundreds, if not thousands, of templates to choose from.

They are often known as "Themes"

A template will be a basic pre-set layout for your site.

They usually can be modified to suit your tastes.

Your choice of template should be dictated by the kind of business you are doing.

If you are doing a mainly shopping-based site, then you are going to want to use a template that allows you to showcase your products.

Makes sense, right?

You would be surprised how many sites will use templates more suited to other types of ventures, such as blogging, just because it looks cool.

You have to choose your template by your criteria.

If you are doing a shopping-type site, then use a site that showcases your products, loads fast, and does not have needless clutter.

Some templates will have lots of cool options and sections.

But does your business need them?

As much as sites with "Bells and whistles" can be cool to look at, they can also be slow loading, especially on mobile devices.

Have you ever clicked on to a site and been met with a slow loading page.

How long before you clicked back off because you couldn't be bothered waiting or didn't trust the site?

A few seconds most likely.

People are impatient for one.

Secondly, people distrust slow loading sites because bad sites often load slow as they put malware on your device.

Your site may be secure as possible, but if it's a slow loader, it doesn't look good or promote trust.

Also, page load speed is a factor in search engine optimization (SEO).

I will get into SEO in its own section, but basically, there is a criteria that search engines, such as Google, use to rank sites in results.

Slow loading pages equal a bad user experience

This can hurt your rankings, if only to a minor degree.

If it can be avoided by choosing the correct template, then why not?

On the other hand, if you are going to be primarily blogging, perhaps an author or an affiliate marketer, then you don't need a site that has all kinds of features to show products.

A lot of templates can actually be hybrids.

Again, don't choose a template purely because it looks cool.

Research what it's actually built to do.

You may also find that the designer has made three variants.

One for shopping, one for more information-based sites, such as blogging, and a hybrid.

As I said earlier, I actually encourage shopping sites to have some kind of blogging presence for promotional purposes.

But, if you do not intend to blog at all and just showcase products, then why get a template with the feature?

Keep your site easy to navigate.

It can be very tempting to have all kinds of options on your site menu.

Which, if relevant and useful, is a good thing.

But ensure that your users can find everything with ease via the menu.

Keep things organized.

Do not be tempted to overload your site with excessive amounts of pictures or crazy color schemes.

It's surprising to see how many sites will use red text on a white background for example.

This can be very hard on the eyes, or even hard to read, on mobile devices.

Keep to black text on a white background or vice versa.

Sure, perhaps a colored headline here and there if it suits your needs.

But large walls of red text on white background, or using a crazy font, is honestly not a good idea at all.

What looks good on a large desktop screen may look terrible on a mobile phone screen.

Be sure to test both versions before you commit to settling on a design.

Too many pictures can not only look cluttered, it can also lead to slow loading times.

Use pictures because users love visuals, but don't go overboard.

If your software allows, use image size reducing software.

A 400kb picture file can be reduced to 70kb, for example, and not lose any of its clarity.

If you have three pictures on your page, 210kb is far better than 1.2mb (1200kb) when it comes to page loading times.

I personally advise against "Pop-ups"

Some sites will use pop-ups to try and get you to sign up for newsletters.

They are usually set to appear 10 seconds after you turn up on the site.

Sometimes 5 seconds.

I hate them, and so does everyone I know.

How do I know if I want to read more of your content by subscribing to your newsletter, if I have only been on your site 5 seconds and read maybe two lines of your work?

It honestly puts me off the site and I never sign up on principle.

If they blast me that quickly with a pop-up, god knows what my inbox will look like if I do sign up.

See my point?

If you do choose to use "Pop-ups" to promote your newsletter, set them at a reasonable timeframe.

If you have a long article that might take five minutes to read, set it to pop-up after two or three minutes.

If you have a shopping site with a page full of products, then set it for 30 seconds.

Give people a chance to look at what your site is about so they at least have time to develop an interest.

Personally, I advise putting your newsletter opt-in form in a sidebar or at the bottom of pages, rather than thrusting it into your viewer's face.

Interesting content.

Keep your content interesting and relevant.

If you have a shopping site, as I said, consider doing a blog to showcase your latest or upcoming products if you think it will be beneficial.

Do posts about your company and any events you may be having.

I will get into promotion further on in this guide, but be sure to create content that people will find interesting or helpful.

You may post a maintenance guide on looking after your products post-purchase to keep them in peak condition.

A troubleshooting guide for new users.

Again, interesting and useful.

Take into consideration what I said about layouts.

Make your content easy to find and easy to navigate.

Put information in order and make it easy to find from the menu.

You may have created a troubleshooting guide as a blog post, but, put a link to it on your main menu or in your sidebar as a quick reference point.

If someone is looking for the guide they may not think, or want, to trawl through your blog post feed looking for it.

Have your contact page on your menu.

Sometimes customers, current or prospective, may want to ask you a question directly.

Put all your contact details on one page.

I have seen sites that put their contact page link at the bottom of pages as part of a secondary menu.

My advice is to put it on the top menu in plain sight and easy to navigate to.

An about page can also be a useful feature.

Write a little bit of information about your company.

Where you are based, when you started, what your aims and company mission are.

You would be surprised at how many people may visit a site, be unsure on whether to trust putting their card details in, but look at the about page and see information that builds trust enough to purchase.

If you are an affiliate marketer/blogger or author, the same applies.

Put an about page with some details about you.

For example, you may be an affiliate marketer that promotes tech goods.

You may write that you have ten years of experience in tech and used to work at so and so.

This will make readers trust your product recommendations more, and therefore be more likely to click through your links and purchase.

Don't lie or fluff things out!

Tell the truth.

If you do not have ten years of experience, and never worked a day in your life in the tech field, do not claim as such.

If you are just someone who loves tech and researches products, then put that.

People will respect that much more and it's the right thing to do.

Consistency

Keep your site up to date with fresh content.

Add new products where possible, or rearrange and refresh featured products.

Perhaps have a product of the week feature or some kind of special deal.

This is so that returning visitors will see that the site is active, and the differences will trigger their interest to see what might be new.

People browse before they purchase.

Encourage them to browse by keeping things fresh and different.

Attract their interest and you have their focus.

This focus and interest will be on your products.

This is how sales are made.

If you are a blogger/affiliate marketer/author, then try to post new blog posts on a consistent basis.

Daily is of course optimal, but several times, or even once a week, is not terrible.

Just try not to be too sporadic and leave large random gaps between posting.

I know this from experience.

I have had sites where I have been posting three times a day for two weeks, got distracted by another project for a week and half, then returned to check my stats and found my traffic was consistent and rising steadily, but then plummeted a few days into me not posting.

On some of my sites, I now opt to put my articles as static pages rather than blog posts.

The reason for this is that I may not want, or need, to create a constant stream of articles.

I may just create a new article page when and I have new information to post.

People like fresh blog content, and if they like your site they will return daily or at least every few days.

If they visit several times and see that you have no recently dated blog content, they will stop coming to your site in short order as something else will grab their attention or they think your blog is "dead"

If they see from the off that your site is a fixed set of pages, then they may just browse everything they want in one sitting.

This can, but not always, lead to a sale that day rather than in the future when you have written fresh blog posts that may be the tipping point for them.

The reason is that with a blog they may just read the latest two or three posts.

This may be not enough to tip them into buying something.

If they realize that all the information on the site is already there, they may read it all in one go, and this may enough information in one sitting to tip them.

Keep your content fresh and consistent as much as possible.

Update static pages and even old blog posts when you have new relevant information.

Step 7 – The basics of SEO

OK, so now we get into some technical stuff.

I can't cover this topic in advanced detail, as it is far too broad and constantly evolving, but I can give you the basics.

SEO is Search Engine Optimization.

Google, Bing, Yahoo, are examples of search engines.

Optimization is the practice of making your site meet the criteria to rank highly in search engines.

It is said that the Google search algorithm has 200+ points in its criteria when it ranks a piece of content.

The truth of this is open to debate.

Google does not make its criteria public because it leaves the algorithm open to the exploitation of loopholes.

In the old days, to get ranked top in search results was actually very easy.

If your domain had the right keywords and your content had enough keywords and backlinks.

You would rank top in search results quickly and easily.

If Jim had managed to get hold of discountgaminglaptops.com, filled his site with content that was saturated with the words "discount gaming laptops" and he submitted his site to some blog directories.

He would be at the top of google search results for "discount gaming laptops" and he would be very hard to budge by competitors.

Those days are long gone.

If Jim got hold of that domain today, saturated the content with keywords, and blasted his link all over directories, he may not appear in rankings in the first 20 pages of results or more.

Google hates such practices now.

Now, the domain name is not anywhere near as much of a major factor.

Keywords have to be used in a relevant and sparing amount, and submitting to site directories is frowned upon, to say the least.

Such directories are classed as link farms and will often count against the site as a negative.

Some may disagree with some of what I have said, but try the old methods and see how you get on in comparison to the new methods.

Despite all the courses and promises of "secret techniques" online, let me tell you the overall key to SEO these days, and any days going forward unless there is some revolutionary change.

Create relevant and fresh content.

Use keywords in a natural fashion.

Provide a good user experience.

Have good page load speeds.

Aim for social interaction.

You follow that criteria and you will discover that you will do fine.

I'm sure there will be people who are SEO experts screaming at that statement and talking about "Meta tags" and "H1, H2" blah blah.

Listen.

The truth of the matter is, it really all depends on the above factors above all else.

I have created sites that I spent ungodly amounts of time optimizing in a tech fashion.

All kinds of details looked at and tweaked.

Courses followed, videos watched, techniques implemented.

Ridiculous amounts of hours on each piece of content.

Some ranked well for keywords, and some did not.

I have done other sites that I just put together using the above criteria.

Some content ranked highly, some did not.

So, you tell me.

What is best?

Obsessing and stressing over all kinds of small techniques and details for hours at a time?

Or following a base criteria, and getting similar results?

Two things will predominately dictate the ranking of your content.

The keywords you are chasing and the trust/authority of your site.

Bottom line.

A well-established site, with years of history, content, and social interaction built up, can post an inferior piece of content compared to a new site and still outrank it

SEO experts will scream, "No but…"

No, it's an established fact in my eyes.

I, and many others, have created great optimized content full of information on a newish site, or even a site with some age and content, and been far down the rankings compared to a thin piece of slower loading content on a long-established site.

I have done research in search results for competitive keywords and seen other sites have the same issue.

Certain big dogs dominate certain keywords no matter what quality of content they put up.

Some established sites can post 200-word articles and dominate keywords, and a newer site can post a 2500+ word article (The often touted magic number Google loves) and not even get in first 5, or even 10 pages.

Feel free to have a look around Google, you wil find plenty of examples.

Create relevant and fresh content.

Keep your content relevant to what you are talking about and make it informative to your readers.

If you are talking about a topic, stay on topic and cover it in as many useful details as is needed.

Do not ramble for the sake of it, and do not skimp and half bake it.

Keep the information up to date and even revisit information periodically to update it.

If you do this, and readers enjoy it, they will share it and most likely read more of your content.

Another aspect of SEO is what is known as "Bounce rate"

If a reader goes on your long page, only reads a sentence or two, then clicks off, "Bounces" that actually is a signal to Google that they didn't like your page or found it irrelevant to what they were looking for.

If they take time to read it and share it.

Must be relevant and the user enjoyed it.

It will count in your favor.

Again, if anyone doubts that, look at top ranking pages that have thin content, but lots of comments and shares.

Then look at pages with masses of information, no comments, and no shares.

See where they rank in comparison.

They may still be on the first page of results, but they won't be top.

Surely the fully optimized lengthy page should rank better?

The truth is much different, as you are free to research.

Keep it relevant and provide a good user experience.

The shares and comments will do the rest.

Use keywords in a natural fashion.

To refresh your memory from earlier.

A keyword, or keyword phrase (also known as long-tail keywords) are the words used to find things in search engines.

So, Jim would want to rank for "Discount gaming laptops" as his main keywords.

The competition for that term would be extremely fierce and most likely well-established sites would dominate the search term results.

But, Jim can target more specific terms in order to rank for those,

For example, if Jim created a page and targeted the keywords "Black gaming laptops for under $1000" he may stand a far greater chance of ranking in search results.

This is actually better for Jim.

Because although the number of searches for that term may be far less than "Discount gaming laptops", guess what?

The customer is further along in deciding what they actually want.

Instead of them searching for a large selection of laptops to browse, they already have a criteria and price range for what they are looking to purchase.

Make sense?

The same can be said for supplements.

Someone searching for "Fitness supplements" is more about browsing at that point.

Even if they find something they like, they may go off and read reviews elsewhere online and end up purchasing it through a link on that site, or start shopping for prices online.

If someone types in "Low caffeine vegan pre-workout supplements" they are shopping for specific items.

When creating your content, try to use keywords that are more specific to a purchasing customer rather than a browsing one.

Although the big dogs may dominate the common searches, they often do not target the specifics.

This is how you can create content that ranks and produces money, rather than trying to battle the big established sites for generic keywords.

When you create your content, do not lash the keywords all over the place.

Keep them relevant and natural.

Too many and Google will think you are keyword stuffing like the old days.

Too few and Google will not see the content as relevant.

Make sense?

Just write naturally and aim for specific terms that a customer would use, rather than generic ones that browsers will use,

Provide a good user experience.

I have covered this already, but just to overview.

Just make your pages and overall site easy to navigate and enjoyable to use.

Don't cover it in pop-ups and load it with needless pictures or information.

Make it easy to find in menus and also link to other useful information.

For example, if you have a site that sells candles, then suggest other ranges they may like.

If you have a page on vanilla scented candles, then link to your page on chocolate scented candles.

Think of your online store, like a store.

Instead of strolling around, they scroll around.

They don't change aisles, they move to other pages.

Don't crowd your pages and keep products in a logical order.

If people can find what they want, they stand a chance of buying.

If people enjoy your site, they stand a chance of sharing it with friends and followers on social media.

This all helps with SEO.

Have good page load speeds.

Again, I have covered this already, but to refresh.

Don't clutter up your pages with needless content or "Add-ons" that slow your page down.

It creates a bad user experience and also causes bounce.

Again, bad for SEO.

Aim for social interaction.

Let's say, for the sake of debate, social interaction is not a major factor in SEO.

Is it still not better for people to see your site with an active comments section on posts?

It shows you actually care about your customer's opinions and questions.

Can more social media shares lead to more traffic, potential sales, and even more potential social media shares?

Of course!

The more likes and shares a post gets, the more they are likely to attract even more.

That is how viral posts often occur.

People see something is trending, take a look, and often click the like or share for the sake of it.

Not all, but enough people do.

It all helps to get your content in front of people.

Now, let's say it is a factor in SEO.

See my point?

I'm sure that section would cause many SEO experts to throw their arms in the air and start on with all kinds of tech jargon.

But I assure you.

Those basic steps will do you no harm.

As I said, there are advanced techniques that will teach you all kinds of terms, optimization methods, etc.

But rest assured.

When all the fat is trimmed away.

Those steps are the core of it all.

Step 8 – Promotion

In this part, I am going to give you some basics on how to promote your online business.

Search Engines

In the section above we looked at that topic in a decent amount of detail.

But just to surmise.

You can lots of traffic and customers directly from search engines.

It is no secret that when people are looking to make a purchase, even at a traditional offline store, they will often research online first.

For information, reviews, and of course, price comparison.

As I said above, if you get your site, or at least some of your pages, ranking in search engines for specific search terms. You will get traffic, and therefore potential customers.

Your site, if it is a branded domain, will most likely rank top for its name anyway.

This is why I said to make it memorable.

For example, Jim may not rank top for "discount gaming laptops" but he will almost certainly rank top for "Jim's discount gaming laptops"

So long as Jim's domain is memorable, repeat customers, or people who may hear of the site, will find it with ease in search results.

As long as he follows the steps I mentioned above, he will rank for his own search term.

Now, if you are dead set, or get advised, to take an SEO course, then go for it.

There is a lot of information I have not covered in this book when it comes to SEO.

As I said above, this is not meant to be an all-inclusive techies guide to online business.

But, I would lay a wager that, when all is said and done, you will find that the core aspects I taught you above, are what counts.

Courses will teach you the technicalities, no doubt.

You will learn all kinds of terms, techniques, and skills.

They will help you rank for harder keywords.

But.

It will not be cheap to take these courses, and it will not be a quick learning curve.

It will also not guarantee results.

Some keywords are so dominated by established sites that you basically stand no chance of taking the top slots from them.

I'm sorry, but it's true.

For example.

If you started a news website and wrote thirty articles every day.

Do you think you will EVER outrank sites such as the BBC, CNN, etc, for the search term "News"?

The same applies to some terms that may be related to your business, according what field you are in.

If you do fitness supplements, don't expect to own that search term.

But, as I said.

You can dominate more targeted terms, and also build hype around your own domain name so that people search you direct.

You can always search online for SEO information and techniques.

Most of what is sold in courses, or as part of membership sites, can be found with a little research, free of charge.

Social Media.

One of the best ways to promote your online business is with social media.

Granted, it is a noisy place, and it can provide mixed results.

But, it can help you get your brand and products out to the masses like no other medium.

A post or video can go viral and have tens of thousands of views, and potential customers, in a matter of hours.

Even low-performing posts and videos can accumulate hundreds, if not thousands, of views over time.

Just because a post only gets 30 views on its first day, it doesn't mean that someone with a large following may not share it 2 weeks later and surge the views up by a thousand overnight.

It happens.

The more posts, videos, etc, you have out there, the more views and potential customers your products/brand will encounter.

Simple as that.

If you have a new product line, then create posts to share on social media.

These can be blog posts, or simply pictures with some simple information, a link to the product page, and some relevant hashtags.

Just in case you do not know what a hashtag is I will give a brief description of what they are and how they are used.

A hashtag looks like this #

Think of it like a keyword.

So, if you were posting a picture and link to a new protein powder you have in stock, you may use hashtags such as these.

#fitness #supplements #fitnesssupplements #proteinpowder #health #healthandfitness

Things along those lines.

The reason is this.

I will use Twitter as an example.

On Twitter, people can search for #

This is why you may see certain # trending.

This means lots of people are using that tag in posts and many more are viewing it.

Most social media platforms, besides showing it to people who search for it, will also show it to people who have that # in their bio.

For example, someone who's into fitness may have #fitness in their bio as a hobby.

So, like keywords, hashtags can get a lot of traffic to your posts and therefore products.

It is also not a bad thing to create your own #

This is really simple to do.

Jim may put the hashtag #jimsdiscountgaminglaptops in his social media posts.

The reason for this is simple.

If someone reads a post with that hashtag, they may either search for it to see more, or click on it and be taken to a feed that contains all posts with that #

Which would be a feed of Jim's posts.

Aim to follow people in your field.

If you have a business-related to candles, then follow people who also do candles, home furnishings and décor, novelty gifts, etc.

There are many benefits to this.

Firstly, they may follow you back and even share some of your posts with their followers.

Also, sometimes people will often look through the followers of the people they follow.

If they spot your account, they may take a look at your feed/products, and perhaps even follow you.

They may end up purchasing, sharing posts, etc.

Don't be afraid to follow your competitors or others in fields related to you.

Keep your posts, interesting, relevant, and consistent.

Social media is awash with posts 24 hours a day.

But, this is in your favor.

It can be awash with YOUR posts 24 hours a day.

This is not to say spam endlessly.

It is to say, if you can post several times a day at varied times, your posts will be working for your while you sleep.

As I said, just because your post only gets 10 views the first day, it doesn't mean that when you check your stats in a week, that it won't have accumulated 400 views.

If you do 5 such posts a day, the views start to add up.

Each post not only stands a chance of you making sales, it can also get shared, or attract new followers.

Make your posts interesting and share-worthy.

Try to include pictures and stay to the point of what you are saying.

For example.

If you do a blog post to promote your new protein powder blend.

Use a catchy headline, maybe "We are celebrating the launch of our new protein powder"

Click here for details.

Put a link to the blog post.

Attach a picture that attracts attention, or one of the actual product.

Put relevant #

It'll do its job.

Don't get the urge to be too sales pitchy in all of your posts.

If you look at that post, it draws the reader in with "just enough" information.

Celebrating…Launch…New

People will be intrigued about what you actually mean by "Celebrating"

Is there a party or launch event they can attend?

Is there a prize giveaway?

"Launch" and "New" indicate it is fresh as can be.

Everyone likes to be first on something new and cool.

There's no sooner than launch.

Most people will click on that link out of pure curiosity.

Others will share it just because it's something new and their friends and followers may be interested.

If your blog post and sales page are good enough, people will purchase it just to see what all the hype is about.

Not all, but some.

Your new protein powder business is rolling.

I mentioned earlier in the book about not getting involved with trolls or debates, and to also interact with your followers.

Represent your business in the best light possible.

Do not get involved in nonsense, and do not disregard any good-meaning questions or comments.

Represent your brand as the company you wish you could deal with.

What I mean by that is, if you were a customer, how would you LOVE to be treated by a company.

Not expect, love.

Provide that service to your customers.

This is not to say let idiots and time wasters run you ragged.

Give people the highest level of professional service possible, and that is how your company will be regarded.

Give people sloppy service or crappy answers, and that's how your company will be regarded.

Sloppy and crappy.

It really is that simple.

Email.

I have touched upon email lists and placing of opt-in forms, so I will just cover the promotional aspect here.

If you are doing a product/shopping business, you should aim to create brochure-based newsletters and send them out periodically.

Do not bombard your subscribers day after day.

Once a week or perhaps bi-weekly will be sufficient.

Most of the services I mentioned earlier have templates for newsletters and brochures.

So, it usually is just a case of selecting one and filling it in.

Ensure to make each new edition exactly that.

A new edition.

Do not just send the same brochure every time.

If you do not have any new products to showcase, then simply use a different template or move things around a little.

Keep it fresh and interesting so they are inspired to look at the products.

Perhaps consider doing special offers on certain products or highlight that certain items are almost sold out.

Again, as with any of the aspects in this course, treat your customers as you would want to be treated.

You would not want to be constantly bombarded, and you would not want to receive the same old newsletter time after time.

Neither do they.

Pay per click marketing (PPC)

This is a mixed bag of tricks in my opinion.

Some people swear by it, I personally do not use it.

I have in the past and did not see it worthwhile based on my results.

Some people are PPC masters.

I am not, and will not claim differently.

PPC is a simple concept on the surface, but somewhat tricky to be successful with.

I'm sure you have seen banner ads on sites or perhaps places like YouTube videos.

They are usually a picture or block of text advertising a product or service.

If you click on them, you are taken to another site where you can purchase the product or service.

When you click on that ad, you cost the advertiser money.

Hence "Pay per click"

The cost is based on keywords.

So, a company may pay $2 per click for say, "Laptops"

When their ad is displayed, it will be displayed on content related to laptops.

A YouTube video about laptops may have banner ads appear for example.

If any viewers click on that banner ad, it will cost the advertiser $2 each, and every, time.

You can also use this service to drive traffic to your products.

The main one is Google Ads.

There are other options and a lot of social media platforms run similar programs with sponsored posts etc.

You pay and your post will be shown as an ad.

The format all depends on the individual platform.

Some will allow you to link to an outside site, such as your product page, and others will allow you to link to your social media account on that platform.

Whatever the case, you will be bidding on keywords and will need to set a daily budget.

To keep it simple.

Let's say you were bidding on the "laptops" keyword at $2 a click.

If you set your budget at $100 a day, then your ad would be shown until you hit 50 clicks. (50 clicks x $2 each = $100 budget)

You pay that whether the person who clicks purchases from you or not.

So, as you can imagine, if your product page does not convert at a decent rate and your profit margin is not adequate, it can be a very expensive venture.

There are two ways to look at it.

Let's say you were selling candles at a $3 profit at $2 per click.

You would need to sell at least 34 candles per 50 clicks just to break even.

But, if you are selling protein powders at a $20 profit margin, you would only need to sell 5 units per 50 clicks to break even.

The people who usually praise PPC are the ones who are often selling items with high-profit margins.

Some internet gurus will sell courses with several hundred dollar profit margins by targeting keywords that cost pennies per click.

So, you can see why they praise PPC.

If your profit is $300 per purchase and you are paying 20 cents per click…

PPC can be effective, but you would have to do a lot of research, and also give careful consideration before getting involved.

I'm not saying don't touch it, but I am saying be very careful.

I personally am not a fan, but you will hear some people praise it to the heavens.

Make your own choices and use caution is my advice.

In the next section, I am going to show you a full step-by-step guide to setting up an online business using the techniques above using affiliate marketing as a background business model.

Even if you do not want to do affiliate marketing and want to do your own products or another business model, the concepts are very similar.

Online Business Example

I have talked a lot about online income, so here I will show you the basics of how to set up an online income stream you can start working on to earn money and to gain online experience.

In this section, you will learn the basics of Affiliate Marketing.

Simply follow through the steps and you will learn the basics of online marketing.

A lot of the information you will find in this course is similar to the kind that is being sold online by Gurus for large amounts of money.

Their courses may be fluffed out and have pitches for "secret" techniques in order to make them appear worth their price tag.

The truth of the matter is you will have to learn the basics before you can even hope to understand the advanced techniques.

Most of these "secret" techniques are often just spins on the basics and are often obsolete within short periods of time.

Once you have the basics of this course completed and understood, THEN, you can consider advanced techniques.

Although at first glance affiliate marketing seems to be a really easy concept, once a beginner actually sits down to start it can be a very daunting prospect.

On the surface it appears all you have to do is join an affiliate program, post some links, and the money magically starts rolling in.

Wouldn't that be marvelous!

I'm sure that if you are reading this, you have seen all the self-proclaimed gurus touting their courses that will make you a millionaire in six months.

Let me tell you this straight off the bat.

They make THEIR millions from selling YOU their courses.

I'm not saying that their courses do not work.

What I am saying is that what they are selling is decorated basics.

Regardless of what techniques they stick on the outside, the core aspects are usually the same.

So, without further delay, let's proceed to step 1.

Step 1 - What Is Affiliate Marketing?

Affiliate marketing is one of the cheapest and most lucrative businesses to get into if performed correctly.

As mentioned above, it really does involve posting links and receiving money if anyone performs a certain action.

This action could be purchasing a product or signing up for a service.

Typically, the affiliate would receive either a percentage commission, recurring payments, or perhaps a flat fee.

Example A.

Sarah creates a blog about skincare and joins an affiliate program for a skincare company that pays 10% commission.

She writes articles about skincare and posts affiliate links within the content that refer the reader to the skincare product website.

Over the course of a month, Sarah promotes her blog on social media and drives a lot of traffic to her articles.

A lot of readers end up reading her articles and clicking through her links.

Some of the readers purchase products through the skincare site after clicking through Sarah's links.

The total sales resulting from Sarah's referred customers ends up being $25,000 at the end of the month.

The skin care site pays Sarah 10% of the total sales she referred.

10% of $25,000 = $2500.

Sarah gets paid $2500.

That is the extreme basics of commission-based affiliate marketing.

Example B.

John creates a blog about learning to trade stocks.

He finds an affiliate program that pays a recurring fee for every person that joins a stock trading membership website.

The membership is $24 a month and it pays the affiliate 50% recurring monthly commission for as long the member continues to pay the monthly fee.

John follows the same strategy as Sarah and posts articles containing the affiliate links while driving traffic to his blog.

Over the course of time, John ends up referring 1000 people who remain members of the stock trading website membership program.

1000 people x $24 = $24,000 per month.

50% of $24,000 = $12,000 per month.

John earns $12,000 per month, every month that his referred people stay members.

As his referred members increase, so does his monthly recurring payment amount.

Example C

Steve creates a blog about financial matters.

He finds an affiliate program that pays a flat fee for every person he refers to a credit card offer.

The referral fee is $150 for every person that applies and qualifies for a credit card offer.

Steve follows the same blueprint as Sarah and John.

He creates a blog, writes articles about financial matters, and includes links to the credit card offer.

At the end of the month, his blog has referred 2000 people through to the credit card offer.

400 people ended up applying and qualifying.

400 people x $150 flat fee = $60,000

Steve receives $60,000 as a one-off payment for that month.

If he manages to do this every month, he will be earning $60k every month!

As you can see affiliate marketing can be very lucrative!

Now before we proceed, I have to address two points of view on this.

That sounds too good to be true!

Well, it is true.

There are people making literally millions of dollars per year from affiliate marketing.

You can doubt that if you want to.

It doesn't change the fact that it's true.

Is this common?

Of course not.

Is it possible?

Absolutely.

But consider this.

Aiming for a goal of replacing your job is perfectly realistic.

People do it every single day.

After reading the above examples do you think that creating perhaps $10k a month online is impossible?

Would you like to do that?

Be able to relax at home, set your own schedule, spend your time your way?

Continue to Step 2.

Step 2 - Choose A Niche.

The first thing you need to do is choose a niche.

A niche is a topic that you intend to specialize in.

This will dictate pretty much everything you do when trying to make money online.

Niches are typically broad or deep.

Examples of broad niches.

Weight Loss

Outdoors

Sports

Financial

Computers

Examples of deep niches.

Weight loss for women over 40

Camping equipment for cold climates.

Baseball equipment for kids.

Money-saving for students.

Best Laptops for music producers.

As you can see, I have cross-referenced the niches.

Each deep niche is a more focused version of the broad niche it relates to.

Why Is This Important?

Simply because most broad niches are hugely competitive if they have any kind of mass-market appeal.

Let's take weight loss as an example to work with.

The global weight loss market is worth multiple billions of dollars per year.

The weight loss market in the U.S. alone is estimated to be worth in excess of $72 billion per year.

As you can imagine, there are some very big players interested in trying to dominate as much of that market as they possibly can.

But, as the big dogs on the block fight over the bulk of the online market via keywords such as "Weight loss", this leaves plenty of room.

This room is to be found in deep niches such as "Weight loss for women over 40" for example.

Granted, and this is only an example, there will still be a lot of competition in this niche.

You stand more chance of competing on that field than the broad field of weight loss.

Now imagine if you drilled down even further and targeted "Weight loss for women over 40 with diabetes"

Still a large market, but with even less competition.

Again, I mention this is purely an example to display the concept.

Chances are that the niche example is still highly competitive, but you get the idea.

But what kind of niche should I do?

Now, this is a moment when you need to do some self-assessment.

You need to be certain of 3 things for yourself.

Ask yourself the following.

What do I know a lot about?

What am I passionate about?

Can I make money from it?

These 3 factors are imperative to your success.

Let's explore all 3 individually.

What Do I Know A Lot About?

If you are going to be promoting products as an affiliate, typically you are going to be doing reviews or informational content.

Without stating the obvious, you need to know what you are talking about if you hope to have any kind of success.

Trust and authority are key to affiliate marketing.

If your content comes over as purely a sales pitch or vaguely researched, then you can guarantee your readers will not trust you or value your opinion.

If they do not trust you or value your opinion, then they are far less likely to click through your links and make a purchase.

If, on the other hand, you develop a reputation as trustworthy and knowledgeable, then you can expect readers to be more likely to click links to products you promote.

Do not lose sight of the fact that as an affiliate, you are an online salesperson.

A lot of people do not like to see it that way, but it's true.

Regardless of you being a reviewer or an informational content creator.

You do affiliate marketing to make money from sales.

But, as with all salespeople, if you do not know what you are talking about or come across as untrustworthy, you will not make sales.

Would you trust a review that comes across as a sales pitch?

Would you take the recommendation of a person who knew very little about what they were telling you to buy?

The key is to keep one thing in mind.

Help people.

People search for reviews and information to solve a problem.

The problem might be what kind of camping equipment is best for their next trip or it could be how to do something.

Your job is to provide the best, most informative, and most reliable solution to their question or problem.

It's a known fact that today the majority of people will research information online when it comes to solving a problem or buying a product.

Obviously, the site that gives them the most informative and honest content will be the one that stands the best chance of the reader clicking their links.

Be honest, be informative, and build trust!

Never forget these key factors.

Pick a topic for your niche that you are knowledgeable about.

One that you are prepared to research in detail each and every time you plan to create content.

Stay on top of all the latest information and do plenty of research before you create content you intend to post.

For example, with products, make sure you actually use the product before doing a review.

You would be surprised how many beginner affiliates just look for the products that pay the most and then create a review based on pushing for sales.

They never use the product and just make it sound as great as possible in order to try and make sales.

Not only is this unethical, it also shows through in their content and ruins trust with the reader.

Have you ever read a review that is basically, "This product is fantastic, it does this, you can buy it here, it does that, and you can buy it there"?

That is most likely a new and inexperienced affiliate desperate for sales that wrote that content.

On the other hand, have you read a review that carefully, step by step, examines the product?

Walks the reader through all the pros and cons of the product, compares them to other similar products, and gives a fair conclusion with a link to purchase.

That is most likely written by an experienced affiliate who knows that *informational content combined with trust equals revenue.*

Ensure you know what you are talking about and only recommend products you truly believe in.

Rule of thumb. If you wouldn't recommend the information or product to a loved one, then do not post it and promote it.

Take time to assess which topic you can create informational and trustworthy content about.

What Am I Passionate About?

Make no mistake, affiliate marketing takes work.

Lots of work.

It doesn't matter whether you are writing articles and reviews, creating videos or e-books, or posting on social media.

Rest assured, you are going to be spending a LOT of time setting up your affiliate marketing business.

Building and maintaining a site.

Managing your social media presence.

Creating content.

Researching products and information.

The list can be extensive according to your business model.

Especially in the early stages.

You have a lot to learn and will make mistakes that have to be rectified.

It may take a period of time before you see any kind of results from your work, if at all.

Now, be honest with yourself.

Are you passionate enough about your chosen topic to spends hours, days, weeks, months, even years, researching and writing about it?

This is not meant to be negative!

This is an honest attempt purely aimed at saving you a lot of wasted effort.

If you choose a topic just because of the amount of money you think you can make, then let me tell you this.

You will not attain great results.

You may get results.

But not great ones.

Why?

Simply put, it is for this reason.

You will not feel like creating content if you are bored or disinterested.

This will show in the content you do create, and it will not create enough enthusiasm in the reader.

This is a sales killer.

It leads to sparse and lackluster effort resulting in weak and rushed content.

It's a simple fact.

Before starting a blog, you should be able to write down at least 50 content ideas that you are fully prepared and excited to produce.

If you cannot do that, then you do not know enough about your chosen topic.

I'm sorry but it's true.

At two posts per week, that's roughly 6 months of content.

If you look at those 50 content ideas and the idea of creating them fills you with dread.

You are not passionate enough to make it a success.

There are plenty of abandoned blogs online that have a handful of posts.

This comes from lack of passion and dedication.

There are plenty of blogs online loaded with content, 100's of posts.

Who do you think made any money?

It's that simple.

Now the key question.

Can I Make Money In That Niche?

You can have a vast source of knowledge and be bouncing with enthusiasm in your chair.

It will be wasted if you can't make any money doing it.

Think about players of a sport.

You have the amateurs who truly love the sport and play it whenever they can.

But they never truly become great or make money from it.

You have professional sports stars who dedicate their lives to their sport and end up making a living, if not a fortune, from it.

Affiliate marketing is no different.

The top affiliates are called "Super affiliates"

They choose a profitable niche and dedicate themselves to being far above all competitors.

It really is the difference between failure, success, and triumph.

But, some sports pay more than others.

A top pole vaulter will make in excess of $100k a year.

A top soccer player will earn 10's of millions of dollars per year.

Both are dedicated to their sports and the best in their niches.

But some sports pay more than others no matter how good they are.

I repeat, affiliate marketing is no different.

The top affiliates in a weight loss niche will dwarf the earnings of the top affiliates in wall clocks.

It's just the way it is.

Now, this is not to say you should not go for less competitive niches.

After all, is it better to earn $100k a year in wall clocks as a top affiliate or earn $30k a year as a reasonable affiliate in the weight loss niche?

After you have decided upon a niche and self-assessed that you have the knowledge and enthusiasm to work at producing quality content.

It's time to research the potential revenue.

You need to take a look around for affiliate programs and also what kind of realistic demand there is in your chosen niche.

I will talk about affiliate programs in the next section.

To assess the potential demand, you simply have to use common sense and do a few internet searches.

The common sense aspect is really simple.

If you are looking to earn a few hundred extra bucks a month, then pretty much any niche is good to go.

If you are looking to make a living or fortune, then you are going to need a large enough pond to fish in and a decent return per sale.

For example, here is a broad niche vs deep niche.

A broad niche of board games probably has quite a few searches and therefore potential customers, but the return is going to be small per sale.

A deep niche of generators is going to have fewer searches but a higher return.

Let's be honest.

Is it better to have 10% on a $30 board game offer and make 2000 sales per year or $6000?

Or.

10% on $1500 generators and make 200 sales per year or $30,000?

In the same vein, is it better to make 3000 broad niche sales that earn you $10 each or $30k a year or to make 100 deep niche sales that earn you $100 or $10k a year?

You want to be in the sweet spot of a targeted niche, that is broad enough to make volume, but deep enough for you to dominate.

It also has to be profitable.

For me personally, if a product cannot produce at least $5 per sale, and cannot result in thousands of sales per year, I won't bother to promote it.

Basically, if I cannot earn at least $10k a year from an affiliate program I will not bother to promote it.

Now, that's not to say I won't promote a program that uses a lot of add-on sales and up-selling to produce revenue for me.

Of course I will!

For example.

Some affiliate programs pay you for everything the customer purchases within 24 hours.

So, if I promote a product that earns me $3, but most customers go on to spend more and therefore drive up my commissions with multiple sales.

Of course, I'm going to promote it.

The first sale may earn me $3, but the add-on sales may earn me another $5, bringing my return to $8 per customer.

In that case, if I'm able to drive 1000's of people per month to the offer, then I'd be a fool not to promote it.

My advice is to find affiliate offers that have either a good return on initial sale or at least good potential for revenue via add-on sales.

You should also take a look around the internet for potential market size.

This can be done with a few Google searches.

You should look for online forums and social media groups related to your niche.

If you find forums with large online communities and social media pages with substantial followings, then this is usually a good indicator of interest and potential revenue.

It will also show you the state of your competition and market size.

If you find a lot of low-quality blogs on your niche topic but large communities and social media followings.

You are in a position to take over and dominate that market if you put in the work that others won't.

If you find well-presented blogs and huge social media followings, then you have a large but competitive market.

You may not dominate it, but you can certainly take a slice.

If you find next to no blog presence and very small social communities, then it's either a small market, low revenue, or both.

The holy grail is a very lucrative market, with a reasonable community size, and no real competitor presence.

If you find such a niche, take it and dominate it before someone else reading this book does.

Step 3 - How To Find Affiliate Programs.

There are affiliate programs for literally any kind of product and service you can imagine.

Weight loss, beauty products, electronics, pony supplies, hotels, car parts, camping gear, golfing products, insurance, credit cards, hamster cages.

I don't care how broad or deep your niche is, there are companies paying affiliates to promote their products.

As we discussed, not all niches are equal in size, and not all products pay big on volume.

But, if you find that niche that you decide can provide traffic and revenue, then you need to look for affiliate programs before proceeding.

Affiliate programs are pretty much divided into two camps.

Both may consist of goods and/or services, but are usually in the following two camps.

Broad selection

Narrow selection

Broad Selection.

Broad selection is as the name suggests.

The site you refer customers to may have a large selection of products for you to promote and also for the consumer to purchase.

Examples of these would be.

Amazon

Best Buy

Walmart

All of the above have affiliate programs and also huge product bases.

This is good for two reasons.

Customer selection and the possibility of add-on sales.

Let's face facts.

How many times have you gone on Amazon for a product and found yourself checking out with several items in your cart?

I know I have, countless times.

If someone had gone to Amazon through one of your links, you would have earned a commission on everything they purchased.

So, a $5 commission ended up being an $11 commission.

That's the beauty of broad-based programs.

Narrow Selection

A narrow-based program may be a specific product that a company specializes in.

Examples of these would be.

Clickbank

Hotels.com

Clickbank is a digital bookseller that pays well and has a large selection of products.

I'm classing it as a narrow niche simply because when you promote a product, it is typically a stand-alone product.

If you are promoting book A, then that's what the customer will be referred to. Nothing else will be suggested and there is no "shopping" aspect.

Hotels.com is typically limited to one trip and although people may shop the site, they typically will buy one hotel package and nothing else for months or years.

Neither of these affiliate programs are bad in any way!

In fact, Clickbank is known to be very lucrative.

Hotels.com is a hugely popular and trusted site.

My point is that the customer either likes the product on offer or they don't.

There's not much chance of getting them into something else.

Someone on Amazon may search for a skateboard but end up buying a T-Shirt and a video game console due to the number of products on offer.

Someone who goes to Hotels.com either books a trip there and then, or they don't.

How To Find Affiliate Programs.

Most companies that have an affiliate program will have a link on their website.

Usually located at the bottom with all their contact information etc.

A lot of the larger companies will either host their own affiliate program directly or will outsource it to professional affiliate networks.

These affiliate networks are companies that are a 3rd party between the affiliate and the product website.

They recruit affiliates into their network and also gather brands into their network for the affiliates to promote.

Typically, these networks will have hundreds of companies and 10's of thousands of affiliates on their books.

This is a winning situation for the affiliates because they have access to top name brands and products.

It's a winning situation for the brands because they have access to a huge base of professional affiliates.

The network company wins because they handle the payments between the affiliates and the companies, taking a cut in between.

This does not affect the affiliate's commission usually.

If a program offers 7% on affiliate sales, that's what the affiliate will earn.

Anything the company pays the network is separate and does not impact the affiliate's earnings.

Three affiliate companies that are well known are.

Commission Junction

Rakuten

Share A Sale

When looking for an affiliate program, either join a network or simply browse some sites you are interested in and look for their affiliate program page.

Step 4 - Research Domain and Keywords.

So, at this point, you have noted what kind of niche you are interested in, and what affiliate programs are available.

Now it's time to research a domain and keywords.

As mentioned above a domain is a web address for your site.

Keywords are what people use to find your content.

Before we look at choosing a domain, we need to consider your targeted keywords.

First of all, you need to consider your niche topic and write down words YOU would search to find relevant content.

For example, if you were talking about affiliate marketing you may have a list of words such as.

Affiliate Marketing

Make Money Online

Learn Affiliate Marketing

Affiliate Marketing Beginners

How To Do Affiliate Marketing

Write down as many as you can think of for your niche.

So now you have a list of keywords.

Enter your keywords into Google one word or phrase at a time.

Take a look at what kind of sites are ranking top in the results.

Are the sites professional and have the writers put a lot of effort into the page to get it to rank so highly?

Is the content detailed or sparse?

Usually, but not always, the more detailed the content, the more competition there is for the keyword.

If someone has taken the time to create a detailed and optimized page, the chances are that the keywords are competitive.

This is usually a decent indicator that sites are battling to be on top of the rankings due to the potential traffic for the search term.

Remember, quality monetized content + traffic = revenue.

Some social media plug-in software will show how many times the content has been liked and shared.

These are usually found at the bottom of the content.

This may display Facebook likes, Twitter re-tweets, Pinterest pins, etc.

If this number is high then it will tell you two things.

The content is considered to be good enough for people to share with friends and followers.

The content is receiving a lot of traffic and therefore potentially a lot of searches.

Obviously, low results will indicate the opposite.

Or at least potentially.

This method is not foolproof, but it is a basic technique that can give you useful information.

If the top results for your keywords have weak content, then it will be a lot easier for you to take their rankings and traffic away from them.

Sound cruel?

Not at all.

*Bear in mind what I said earlier about older established sites holding rank in results with thin content for certain keywords due to large social interaction etc

Remember.

Quality monetized content + traffic = revenue.

I assure you those people will not lose a moment's sleep if they outrank your content and take your revenue.

On the contrary, they will be very happy when the money starts rolling into their bank instead of yours!

Plus, it is better for the site reader if they find good quality content rather than low-quality content.

Domain.

Now you have assessed your keywords, potential traffic, and competition, it is time to consider your domain name.

Ideally, you will be able to buy a domain that will contain your best keywords to enable you to rank high in Google easily.

To be brutally honest, the internet has been running for decades now, so a lot of top domains are either taken or cost a premium.

A typical domain may cost you $15 or so.

A premium can cost thousands.

Do not let this deter you because there are ways around this.

But, first of all, you need to decide if you want to have a purely keyword-based domain or a branded domain.

A keyword domain is exactly what you think.

An example of a keyword domain is **whatisaffiliatemarketing.com**

As you can see it contains keywords and also a targeted question at the same time.

You could do a similar domain based around your niche.

If you are lucky the exact one will be available.

If you are very lucky, it will not be a premium price domain.

Even if it is already taken, or you do not want to pay substantially for a premium domain, there will be very similar ones available.

The other method is to do a branded domain.

This means that you do not focus on keywords, but your brand name.

Your brand name can be anything.

A lot of people either choose a domain that is literally their own name or pick a random word.

The reason for this is it's easy to dominate search results because such words are not usually competitive.

Two good examples of this are Amazon.com and Zillow.com

As you are most likely aware, Amazon is an online shopping site and nothing in the name suggests that.

Zillow is a real estate website and again there is nothing in the name that suggests the site's content niche.

Such a domain name will be very easy to rank for in search engine results, but you will have to learn to drive traffic from other sources until you have built a following.

Once you have been to a domain registrar and selected a domain, you do not need to buy it straight away, just note it down for now.

But I suggest two things.

First of all, if you are set on the domain and are prepared to purchase, then grab it before someone else does.

Secondly, I advise getting private registration and domain protection.

The reason for this is that private registration keeps your personal information private.

If you do not add this, then the domain will be publicly registered to you and that information will be displayed online.

Private registration will give generic information provided by the registrar.

Domain protection stops the malicious transfer of your domain.

In other words, it stops anyone from hijacking and stealing your domain.

Keep your list of keywords, for now, you will need them in an upcoming section of this course.

Step 5 - Set Up A Blog.

Once you have researched your domain and keywords, the next thing is to set up a blog.

A blog is a website that is updated on a regular basis.

Usually composed of a series of articles, it may have a few extra pages of content such as archive pages or product pages.

A static website is created and then rarely updated.

It has fixed content that is not often changed.

A restaurant website would be an example of a static site.

The contact details and menu etc are usually rarely changed.

A blog might be updated, daily, weekly, or monthly.

A static site may be updated a few times a year, if at all.

I have tried quite a few different website/blog creation platforms over the years.

Some, to be quite honest, were a literal waste of time.

I spent large amounts of time learning the software and creating content only to learn that the software had flaws or limitations.

Now, let's get this straight.

There is no perfect web creation software out there.

All have their pros and cons.

It could be too steep a learning curve, clunky interface, conflicting feature issues, all kinds of things.

But, after a lot of trial and error.

A lot.

I have finally settled into using WordPress as my "Go-to" software.

I'm not going to start with a whole review of the software, but I will say that you will save yourself a lot of time and aggravation if you use it.

You will find other software platforms that will appear easier to learn and use, but, after spending time with them, you will find big flaws.

Do your own research to see which platforms you enjoy and are comfortable using.

I will list here the basic steps you need to take after choosing your platform.

This is an overview, not a step-by-step guide to building a blog.

Bear in mind some platforms will require you to own a domain before you can start building your blog.

My suggestion is to try any free trials that use a generic domain, so you can try the platform before committing to buying a domain name.

For the time being, we will assume you have already purchased a domain.

Template.

To begin you will choose a template that reflects how you want your site to look.

Most platforms have a large selection of free and sometimes premium templates.

These templates can be modified to suit your design ideas.

You should give consideration to how you want your site to look, loading times, user experience, and also ease of maintenance.

Obviously, you want your site to look amazing and professional.

You want visitors to look at it and think "Wow, this is nice!"

But, trust me on this.

Do not sacrifice loading times and user experience for aesthetics.

Most people use mobile phones now to view the internet.

If your site has all kinds of cool features it can slow downloading times.

Slow loading times result in quicker bounce rates.

I'm sure you have clicked on to a site that was loading too slowly on your phone and have backed out before it has fully loaded.

Other people are no different.

If your site is not loaded in a few seconds, people will simply hit the back button and go to another site.

Keep your site looking nice, but also on the right side of mobile loading times.

The next factor is user experience.

Too many people try to make complex sites full of cool sections and menus that not only bloat loading times, but can be confusing to navigate.

People want things as fast as possible.

Nobody wants to be clicking endless menus and links trawling your site for the information they came for.

Make sure the site is easy to navigate by keeping it organized in sections and be sure to link to relevant pages within articles so that people can move from information to information with ease.

This also helps with SEO.

Google is very focused on relevant content and user experience, so you should be too!

The next factor is the ease of maintenance.

Just remember, the bigger the site, the larger the amount of work it takes to maintain it.

Think of it like a house.

The bigger it is, the more rooms there are to clean, decorate, and repair.

I'm not referring to the number of posts you make, the more the better.

What I'm referring to is the number of sections.

I have seen sites with endless drop-down menus and cool plug-ins.

*A plug-in is a feature added to a website that adds new features not part of the base software.

They look great, but, all those menus make navigation harder, and all those plug-ins have to be updated and may conflict with each other over time.

All software has updates and so do plug-ins etc. Sometimes plug-ins are not updated till a while after the main software update.

This can lead to conflicts in the coding and crashes or simply non-functioning plug-in based site features.

The more you have, the bigger the risk of problems and headaches for you.

I'm not saying do not use them, you should use them, but I am saying don't pile them up.

Be selective.

Let's assume you have set up your base blog.

Base Features.

You should have these base features on your blog.

You should have your post archives and a follow and contact page.

Post Archives and Categories.

Your post archive will make it easy to find other articles on your site.

If your site has dozens of posts and the only way a user can find them is clicking the "Next" button through article after article, it's a problem.

People have short attention spans and want everything right away.

Your site should cater to this.

If you create categories and utilize them effectively, you will get more time from your readers.

For example, if you have a site on camping gear reviews, then it makes sense to have categories such as "Tents" "Sleeping bags" etc.

Someone is not going to want to read a tent review then have to click "Next" on 8 articles about sleeping bags, stoves, and lanterns, before they get to another tent review.

Add categories, it will make your life easier and lead to a better user experience.

A frustrated user will leave your site quickly.

An interested user will view more of your content and therefore be more likely to click through a link and earn you money!

Archives are a similar concept, but typically based around the date of the content publication.

People may be looking for the most recent information instead of specific topics.

If possible, aim to use both categories and archives.

Content

You should aim to make the best content possible and as often as you can.

Quality first, quantity second.

There's no point in churning out content every day if it is rushed and of low quality.

Better to post awesome content once a week rather than post weak content every day.

It's a fact that a portion of your posts are going to be "filler content".

A lot of people don't like to hear that, but it's true.

There are going to be posts on your site that don't rank in search engines and don't get many views.

There are hopefully going to be posts on your site that go viral.

Now tell me this.

Will you feel great if the content that goes viral is some rushed out post you botched together just to fluff your site out?

No.

You should aim to make every post the best you can do.

That way, no matter which content goes viral or ends up as filler, when it is read, it will reflect well on your site.

Make sure it is researched and accurate.

Also, keep it interesting and informative.

Always write your content with the reader in mind.

Make sure they enjoy your content and want to share it.

Too many people worry about keywords and SEO and sacrifice quality content in the process.

Write to impress the reader and not the search engine.

Now, you may be thinking, so why the focus on keywords then?

Simply put, you have to learn how to balance the two.

Of course, you want keywords in your content in order for it to rank in Google.

But, you also want the reader to enjoy and hopefully share your content with others.

Write everything with the reader experience in mind and stay relevant to your topic.

By doing so, keywords will appear naturally, and you will create great content for your reader.

If done correctly, search engines will pick up on your keywords and readers will share your great content!

Never be afraid to ask your readers to share your content etc.

Just mention it at the end of the content.

You would be surprised how many people will share it with their followers if you simply ask!

Visitor Retention.

You should aim to have a newsletter opt-in mailing list and a social media presence.

If you are producing great content, then you will have people that wish to return to your site to see future content.

The truth is, that people forget most of the sites they visit if they only see them once or twice.

Make sure you encourage them to join your newsletter and your social media.

This allows you to alert your followers to any new content and therefore encourage them to re-visit your site.

The more they visit your site, the more they will trust you.

The more they trust you, the more likely they are to end up clicking through your affiliate links to a product you suggest.

Also, it helps your content get views and perhaps shares to the viewer's friends and followers.

This is how content goes viral.

If you have ten thousand social media followers and 20% share your post to a friend who views.

You have just got 2000 followers who enjoyed your content enough to forward it to more people.

If they then share the post…You get the idea.

The more people that see your content the more chances you have of making affiliate sales.

It's that simple.

Obviously, with social media, you should aim to join as many of the top ones as possible.

However, ensure that you do not overwhelm yourself.

Better to have a few well-utilized platforms than many dabbled with platforms.

If you are going to do something, make sure it's worth doing, and do it well.

In my opinion, the most useful platforms are as follows.

Facebook, Instagram, Twitter, Pinterest.

Of course, there are plenty of others, but the above four are the biggest and most effective in my opinion.

Another platform that you should aim to be on, so long as you are confident on being able to create quality content, is YouTube.

I don't imagine I need to describe this platform for you, so I'll keep it simple.

Few platforms have the viral leverage that YouTube does.

A video can be put up and receive millions of views within a day or two if it goes viral.

YouTube also has a social aspect built-in via channel subscribers.

It allows you to notify people as soon as you post a new video and also offers the ability for followers to share on other platforms very easily.

As far as mailing lists software, I have personally used Aweber in the past.

I have tried several platforms and for me, this one is the best.

But there are plenty of platforms that offer free trials for you to take advantage of.

Step 6 - Monetization.

OK, now the part you have been waiting for.

Making money.

Depending on what your affiliate program offers, you should have access to text links and banners.

I will tell you this now straight from the beginning.

Banners look pretty, but generally, text links convert better.

Unfortunately, some sites get so carried away with banners and pop-ups that most internet users have developed "banner blindness"

Think of when you use a site.

Most times you will scroll straight past any ad banners to get to the content you are looking for.

This is standard practice.

Now, this is not to say that banners are a waste of time.

You just have to utilize them properly as support to your text links.

Personally, when I have mentioned a product, I put a text link, and then the banner underneath.

I have also added banners to the sidebar in the past for some promotions.

These banners on desktop/laptop computers are literally at the side.

On mobile, they tend to appear underneath the article.

My logic is simple.

If the reader is interested in the content, then they recognize the banner when they see it, because I have mentioned the product within the content.

How many times have you been on a site and there are banners unrelated to the content?

If you are reading about dog treats but there's a banner for a laptop offer, are you really going to click on it?

No.

You are there to read about pet-related topics, not searching for a new laptop.

You will skim straight over it.

Also, if you bombard the page with banners, it slows down the loading times and also irritates the user.

Rule of thumb - Keep it relevant.

Place useful banners.

Do not place them just to be greedy or to fill space.

It's better to have two banners with thought-out placement that convert rather than ten banners that just fill up space.

Again, I repeat.

Text links convert better.

If someone is reading your content and enjoying it, they will click on links you provide to learn more.

It's that simple.

Do not write sales pitches.

According to your topic, most times you should avoid sounding like a sales pitch.

This is not to say that you shouldn't mention products that you think the reader will find useful.

After all, that's the whole point of Affiliate Marketing.

To promote products.

But there's a world of difference between promoting a product and pushing a product.

I will suggest products I use and link to them.

I do NOT say…Buy this…click this…quick…now…buy it!

I will suggest a product I know to be worthwhile and link to it.

I typically lean towards products with free trials so my readers can have a look at my suggestions without any kind of commitment or risk.

Obviously with book reviews etc, then there is generally no free trial.

But I will not suggest books I have not read and found useful.

The reader can always view the reviews of other purchasers once they reach the product page and make their decision from there.

Also, try to avoid promoting products you have not used.

Of course, if you have a shoe website with links to hundreds of pairs of shoes, no one expects you to have tried them all.

But, if you are linking to a certain product and promoting it heavily, then you should have experience with that product.

All the products I recommend, I either have used, or in most cases, do use.

If I come across a product I try and I don't like, I do not recommend it to my readers, no matter how much I may potentially earn from it.

Place your links and banners strategically, suggest products you believe in and you will make money.

Ad Revenue

Another way to earn money from your blog, although not classed as affiliate marketing, is advertising revenue.

I'm sure you have been on websites and seen various ads on the page.

With an affiliate banner, you get paid by the customer performing an action such as buying a product or service.

Ad revenue is generated either by the reader clicking on the ad, or in some cases, simply by seeing the ad.

I will divide this into two sections to make this easier to understand.

Clicks

Simply put, anytime a website visitor clicks on an ad on your site, you get a dollar amount.

Yes, that is exactly as you read it.

How it works is, on the surface, pretty simple.

There are ad companies, such as Google Ads, that offer services to companies that want to get their ads out across the internet.

The advertisers join up at Adwords and then create an ad.

They then bid on keywords that trigger the ad to be shown.

These are purely hypothetical numbers for the example, so do not refer to them as accurate.

An advertiser selling camping equipment may bid on keywords and each click by a customer will cost them an amount.

Keyword Examples	Cost Per Click Examples
Camping	$2
Tents	$1.65
Sleeping Bags	$0.80

When I say bid, it is not like an auction.

The advertiser simply puts in what they are willing to pay and whoever is bidding the most will get their ads shown with priority.

Priority may include being put on more desirable sites or simply being put in more prominent spots on the sites.

The ad would be linked to the advertiser's site.

So, anyone who clicks on the ad would leave the original site and be transferred over to the advertiser's site.

Just like a normal link would do.

Views.

Views work the same way, except that instead of paying per click, the advertiser will bid on keywords for 1000 views.

The ads will be shown the same way, but the advertiser will pay for the views, not the clicks.

YouTube uses this model when it plays the advertisements before, during, or after on YouTube videos.

How do you get paid from ad revenue?

As a blogger, you get a portion of the click cost for displaying the ads.

For example, we shall simply use 50/50.

So, if an ad is paying $2 per click, the blogger would get $1 every time someone clicks on the ads.

If an ad is paying $5 per 1000 views, then every time 1000 site visitors see the ad, the blogger would get $2.50.

As you can probably guess, the view model works extremely well on YouTube.

This is why so many people film themselves doing all kinds of things in order to get their videos to go Viral.

Based upon $2.50 per 1000 views, (again I repeat, the number is purely an example), the vid's that get millions of views are worth the effort!

In order for you to profit from this on your blog, you would have to join Google Adsense.

The topic is far too broad to go into detail here and you should research the topic before making it part of your online money-making strategy.

You can also use the opposite side of the equation to drive traffic to your website.

You would create an ad, put in a daily budget, select your keywords, and offer what you are prepared to pay per click.

I will detail this more in section 7 of this course that details ways to drive traffic to your blog.

Creating Your Own Products.

Not classed as affiliate marketing, but it can be utilized in order to create affiliate sales.

The best example of this is E-books.

An E-book is simply a book that can be read on devices such as desktops, tablets such as iPad, and of course on mobile phones.

The E-book market is huge, especially on platforms such as Amazon Kindle

So, as you can guess, that is a lot of people and a huge source of potential.

As an affiliate, you could create an E-book on your topic, and include your affiliate links within the book.

You could put the E-book as a free download on your blog.

When people download it (people love free stuff!) and read it, there is a chance they will click through your affiliate links to make a purchase.

*Bear in mind, some platforms, such as Kindle, do not allow linking directly to affiliate products within the books. It varies from platform to platform, so be sure to research.

Again, this is a huge and detailed topic, far outside the scope of this course.

I bring it to your attention so you can see one of the many very effective ways to affiliate market.

There are many ways to monetize your blog, but the next key is vitally important.

Step 7 - Driving Traffic To Your Blog.

So now you have your blog full of awesome content.

You have added your links and banners.

You have your social media and opt-in mailing list accounts set up.

You are ready to earn money!

No one visits your site....

Make no mistake, you can have the greatest site on the internet, but if no one sees it then you are going to earn nothing.

Once you have learned how to set up the basics, then you get to the absolute core element of affiliate marketing.

Traffic.

No traffic, no point.

It's as simple as that.

A terrible-looking site with high traffic will always earn more than a great-looking site with low traffic.

It's just a fact.

But, of course, a great site, correctly optimized for affiliate links, with high traffic, will far outperform the terrible site.

So, here I will give a basic overview of how to drive traffic to your site.

Some I have mentioned earlier in the course.

SEO

As I mentioned earlier, you should aim to rank as high as you can in search engines in order to attract visitors from search results.

This is achieved by creating keyword-relevant quality content.

Write relevant, useful, and interesting content for your readers.

Include keywords naturally, do not overload them just to try and rank in search engine results.

This is called "keyword stuffing"

Google hates it and it also makes your content look spammy to readers.

Just write naturally and stay on topic.

The keywords will place themselves.

Another aspect is back-links.

In the old days, you could attain search engine rank by placing back-links to your site in as many places as possible on the internet.

This led to people spamming links all over comment sections on other sites and even link farm sites that would charge people to post a link.

Obviously, the search engines eventually had enough.

Although backlinks are still relevant, they are not as crucial as they once were as far as search engine rankings.

Do they help?

Yes.

Are they as important as they once were?

No.

You should view back-links as they were originally intended.

Links to enable web traffic to find your content.

They were not intended to convince search engines that your site had the most links and is therefore the best site to visit.

Place your back-links on content that is relevant to your content.

In other words, if you are a member of a forum on pet care, and you have a pet care website, then of course put a link in your forum profile, etc.

If, however, you are a member of a pet care forum, but have a site about sneakers, then is it really relevant to the forum members?

Sure you can put it there if you like, but will you really get any beneficial traffic?

Probably not.

If you start spamming your sneaker link in posts and comments all over the pet care forum, you may not be too popular.

Write naturally and backlink naturally.

Social Media.

You should ensure you have a link to your blog in your social media profiles.

People are obsessed with social media these days.

Next time you are outside just take a look at how many people you see staring at their cellphone.

The vast majority of the time they are on social media.

Leverage this to the best of your ability.

You should use your social media posts to post links to your blog content.

Although some people will advise you to put your affiliate links straight into your posts, it's a debatable practice.

Sure, it can work.

Some social media platforms are fine with you doing that, others will ban you for it.

Some affiliate programs encourage you to do it, others frown upon it.

I look at it like this.

How many people are going to click on affiliate links you happen to spam out all over their social media feeds?

What are you more likely to click on.

"Buy this now!"

Or

"Read my honest review on product x"

Link to your content, it will pay off better.

Plus, most people will follow you for interesting content, few will follow you to be bombarded with product links all day.

As always, provide quality content and you will be far more successful than just hollow sales pitching.

With social media create content that people are willing to do two things for you in return.

First of all, you want them to follow you.

The more followers you have the more chance you have of some of them sharing your content with their followers.

It's purely a numbers game.

Also, larger follower accounts tend to attract more followers.

If a person sees an account with thirty thousand followers, they are more likely to follow than if the account has a hundred followers.

Secondly, you want them to share your content to their followers.

Besides the chance of them clicking on your links there is the chance of them resharing your content to their followers also.

Create content people want to share and also "Like".

Likes will encourage the platform you are on to show your content to more people.

For example, on Twitter, the more likes and retweets a post gets, the more the Twitter algorithm will show it in public feeds.

This is why you will see YouTubers making a point of asking viewers to hit the thumbs up and to, of course, subscribe.

You will also notice that on review videos they will have an affiliate link in the description section of the video.

Ever heard them say, "There's a link in the description" after mentioning a product or reviewing one?

An affiliate link in a lot of cases.

Paid Advertising.

Pay per click or any variation can be very effective if done correctly.

It can be very costly if done wrong.

Pay per click is simply paying for ads that are aimed at specific keywords and each word has a cost per click.

So, let's say you had an ad campaign running for rabbit care.

Each time a web user clicks your ad and gets driven to your site, you will pay a few cents.

You would set a daily budget, let's say $100, and the click cost would be taken from your total.

So, if your keyword "Rabbit care" costs you 10 cents per click, then you would potentially get 1000 visitors to your site per day.

If 20% converted in affiliate sales from your site, 200 people, and they earned you $5 per sale, then you are in good shape.

200 people x $5 = $1000…A 10 x return on your $100 investment.

Good times!

However.

Let's say your topic was "Debt" and you are paying $10 a click for that keyword (Some keywords cost way higher).

You will get 10 visitors a day.

Either you are going to need a site that converts like crazy, an offer that pays a large commission, or best of all, both!

Because if not, you are literally burning through money for nothing.

Paid advertising is very lucrative, but takes a lot of experience and research for it to be an effective option.

I strongly suggest any new marketers stay away until they have some significant experience.

The main, and most popular platform, is Google Adwords

There are plenty of ways to get traffic to your content.

Be creative!

This is just a brief overview, but enough to get you started with driving traffic to your content.

Never stop researching for new techniques and platforms.

New platforms spring up all the time and the early bird catches the worm as they say.

If you can get a presence early on an up-and-coming platform, you will dominate your niche on there before any competitors even turn up.

Course Conclusion

You have finished the basic course.

The course was designed to give you an overview of the affiliate marketing industry and introduce you to what is involved.

If you follow the parts of this course, you have the foundations needed to build an online presence that could potentially produce money.

Each of the steps would of course need more in-depth research on your part and be shaped into your vision of what you want your affiliate business to look like.

But you do have the overall format needed to set up your presence.

Online retail is starting to take significant chunks of sales away from traditional offline stores and malls.

More people are shopping online and often find products on social media or review pages.

The scope of potential for affiliate marketing in the future is staggering.

The affiliate marketing online market share is growing year over year.

As competition between online retailers increases so will the need to have generous affiliate programs in order to attract traffic.

Companies will be turning to affiliates to help drive traffic to their products.

The people who choose to get educated and set up their online presence will be able to cash in on the online gold rush.

The time to learn and start, is now.

The techniques you learned in this online course can be applied to most online business ventures.

Although you may not be interested in making an online business your main venture, you should consider the fact that any extra revenue generated can be put into investments such as dividend stocks for example.

Assets Vs Liabilities.

A key aspect of life is the ability to discern the difference between assets vs liabilities.

This applies to everything I allow into my life.

Actions, purchases, people, everything.

It's a simple concept, yet so many people fail to grasp it let alone utilize it.

If I am going to perform an action, I look at the return on the investment of time and resources.

Time is a precious resource.

If you are going to put your time into something, quite simply, is it going to reward you, or simply drain the time you invest?

Could you invest that time into something more beneficial?

This is not to say, you should not spend time doing enjoyable things that may not yield a financial return.

Spending time resting, doing fun things or unwinding can be just as beneficial as working on your income, etc.

If you are feeling tired, then it would be wise to invest time in resting, because the return on investing that time would be you feeling more energized and focused.

Too many people throw themselves so deep into their work, that they feel worn out and therefore do not operate at their full potential.

Before performing any action, you should consider the return and possible consequences.

If there is a cost to anything, then consider what its return may be.

If it will cost more than it will return, then simply do not do it unless it is necessary.

Consider consequences carefully.

Sometimes helping someone, or even allowing them in your life, can yield consequences.

Some people are simply a liability to themselves and everyone around them.

I'm sorry, but it's true.

I have had some people in my life, that I really liked and enjoyed having around.

However, their actions, and therefore consequences of those actions, simply made them a liability to have around me.

I had to cut them out of my life.

In most cases, it was not actually financial consequences, usually drama, or just being downwind of their stupid choices.

So, eventually, I just considered them a liability that was not worth the investment of time and resources.

Some of you may be horrified and think this is a mercenary approach to life.

I ask you to consider this.

A friend may be fun and the life of the party, but if you are constantly guiding them away from the consequences of their stupid actions to the point where it is causing you trouble.

A point will be reached where you should consider the fact that you are an asset to your friend and a liability to yourself.

If you can detect that point ahead of time, the earlier the better, then you will find you will only have good solid people around you and your life will become far easier.

The same can be said of purchases.

Give careful consideration to any purchases.

Obviously, do not spend twenty minutes weighing up the pros and cons of buying a chocolate bar.

That's simple, it'll taste good for the duration, and will add calorie intake as a consequence.

Not a big deal.

So long as you value the taste enough to work it off at the gym.

I'm talking about larger purchases.

Take, for example, an expensive car.

Most people will think, "Ok, that car's cool, I want it."

Truth be told, the real reason they want that car in most cases, is because they will feel good driving it and will feel good when people pay compliments or look at the car.

The consequence of that action is that they now have a car that requires more costs in maintenance, insurance, etc.

If, in that person's mind, the return of feeling cool and acquiring stares or compliments from strangers is adequate when weighed off against the cost consequences.

Rest assured they will buy it.

If a person with a different mindset looks at the purchase, they will reach far different conclusions.

I will look at the car, think it looks cool, but will also realize that it's going to cost me a lot of money every year simply for owning it, and it will depreciate every mile I put on it.

The consequences far outweigh the benefits in my mind.

I don't care about the opinions of strangers, and do not crave praise from people I do not know.

Now, if it was a car that I had always dreamed of, a goal, and I was able to purchase and maintain, then achieving a goal is not a bad thing.

I don't think like that if the truth be told.

So long as I have a decent car that performs its job, then I'm happy.

I would sooner have a decent car parked outside a great home, than a great car parked outside a decent home.

That is just my mindset.

Everything and everyone should be weighed up as an asset or liability.

Beneficial or detrimental.

As I said at the start of this book. I am not trying to lay out am exact blueprint on how to build wealth.

I am trying to show you the mindset behind it.

To illustrate the concept that I'm trying to portray, I will list a few aspects.

A friend who encourages you to go to the gym is an asset.

A friend who encourages you to get trashed every weekend is a liability.

A family member who encourages you to succeed and who mentors you is an asset.

A family member that is constantly negative to your ideas and who dismisses even talking about it is a liability.

A luxury watch purchase that may attract new clients to your business is an asset.

A luxury watch purchase that is made purely to impress random strangers is a liability.

A day unwinding to recuperate and to take a well-earned break to enable better work tomorrow is an asset.

A day spent lounging on the couch just because you don't feel like working is a liability.

Spending time on social media to build a following to create revenue streams for your business is an asset.

Spending time on social media just being nosey on friends lives, or to show off your own life, is a liability.

The concept is to only have things that are advantageous to you.

This can be actions, items, or people.

They are assets or liabilities.

Give Back.

I truly wish you all the greatest success in life.

I hope that everything you aspire to do is achieved, and far greater success follows right behind.

When that happens, I want you to remember to do something.

Give back to the world.

The world is a mixed bag of tricks.

There are wealthy people who are prolific philanthropists.

There are wealthy people who are greedy and very miserly with their wealth.

Some regular people donate their time to helping the unfortunate of the world.

Other regular people regard such problems as "Not my problem."

There are good-natured kind people, and there are utter selfish scumbags.

For every person smiling right now, there is someone weeping.

Someone's best day of their life falls on the same date as the worst day of someone else's.

It's just the way it is.

I'm of the firm belief that if people spent just a portion of the time they spend watching T.V. actually helping and doing good in the world.

We would all be vastly better off, and the world would be a far better place.

Can you imagine all those millions of hours wasted by the people in your country simply watching television each year?

Take a moment to consider what those millions of wasted hours could achieve if applied to helping to make the world a better place.

Unfortunately, that is not how people think, and therefore, not how the world works.

But, there is something we can all do.

It was Gandhi who said, "Be the change you wish to see in the world."

That is what more people should aspire to.

We have discussed at length ways to improve ourselves and our lives.

Is it really too much to ask for us all to help others do the same?

I'm not suggesting that you should donate an evening a week helping out at a homeless shelter or volunteering at the dog rescue.

If you can, and want to, then fantastic!

Do what you feel is best.

What I am suggesting is that we have spent considerable time looking at ways to generate wealth from the crash.

As much wealth, and as high a standard of living, as we possibly can.

Is it too much of a stretch for me to suggest donating some of that fortune to help the less fortunate?

If you do not have the time, or perhaps simply do not want to donate time, then surely it's not too much to ask for you to help fund those that do donate time.

I can pretty much guarantee that there are multiple good causes in your area that are crying out for donations.

Do a little research online and find out which charities and other good causes may be operating in your area.

Pick one, or more if you want to, good causes you can help.

If there is nothing in your area that strikes a chord with you, then research online for causes that do.

I'm not saying that if you set up a business that earns you a million a year that you should give half to charity.

I am saying that if you spot a cause that touches your empathy and you can donate an amount each month, then why not?

A hundred dollars per month may not touch your income.

It may make a significant difference to a local charity, and therefore touch the lives of multiple people by default.

My personal two charities of choice are related to fighting childhood cancer and helping animals.

I give what I can, when I can.

So, to conclude this section I would simply like to add this:

Do what you can to make the world a better place and do not let success go to your head.

We have more than enough crappy selfish people in the world.

We do not need anyone else joining in.

You have the mindset to change your life for the better.

Use that same mindset to help change the lives of others for the better.

Conclusion

So, there you have my standpoint.

I have told you what I think will happen, why it will happen, and how it will potentially happen.

Make no mistake, we are going digital.

I don't care where you live in the world, it's coming for us all.

When I first heard about Bitcoin well over a decade ago, I remember how averse people were to the concept.

"Digital money, pfft, yeah right"

But I also remember saying to friends and family, "at some point, they will have us all on digital money"

Let's be honest, it's a government's wet dream.

To be able to track every single penny and tax everything possible with ruthless efficiency.

Why wouldn't they be in favor of it?

Personally, I'm not against it.

Do I value privacy, etc?

Of course.

But I also think that being able to hinder nefarious groups and people up to no good is important too.

But regardless of what I, you, or anyone, thinks, it's coming anyway.

As I have said, Google about the official digital currencies.

Google "the digital Dollar" or "digital Yuan" or whichever of the main currencies you wish.

You will find official information about them coming.

For example, the digital Euro has a page on the European Central Bank website and the digital Pound has a page on the Bank of England site.

They are quite open about what they are doing.

But have you seen it in the mainstream media yet?

Not a whisper.

They also say that they will not replace cash, but work alongside it.

But you will see plenty of talk in the mainstream media about "cashless societies" and their benefits.

The public is slowly being warmed up to the idea.

That's why I think Bitcoin has been not only allowed to exist, but actually hyped in the media.

After all, consider the fact that Bitcoin allows people to move money around anonymously.

Doesn't that go against all kinds of laws that apply to cash and even bank accounts?

Yet, Bitcoin has been allowed to do its own thing and even praised via the media for around a decade.

Only recently, now the official coins are almost ready, is it starting to be scrutinized by authorities and the media are starting to mention "nefarious groups" using the coin to move money around.

Think about that and make what you will from it.

Because ten years ago, hardly anyone was interested in digital currencies, and most were even against them.

Now they are part of daily life.

Bitcoin has been an interesting test subject.

Put it that way.

But, I think its usefulness is coming to an end.

I wrote this book to try to help people to see what is coming and to avoid getting caught up in the same trap as the "hashtaggers" and their followers.

Also to try to get people to take their own financial security into their own hands and get new investors to approach investing properly as far as how to think about moves rather than relying on hashtags and hype.

We all saw how that panned out with the China ban debacle.

As I said, I warned people that government bans were potentially coming on May 1st.

It was a simple logic I applied to realize that.

As I have stated.

New official currencies coming, tax concerns, inflation, all the things in this book.

Hopefully, you will see my point and learn from this book in order to set yourself into a good position for when the time comes and they introduce the new currencies.

I simply can't see it being a smooth and incremental transition.

So, I expect chaos on the horizon.

That is where profit is made.

If I am wrong, then I'll still be in a good position.

If I am right, then I will be in a great position.

The crash will come and go.

Things will recover.

It's just going to be a very rocky road as we go through the transition.

You may disagree with some of the things I've said in this book, but my intention is to help as many people as I can at least consider what is coming and what they should do.

Take what you will from this book, do your research and plan as you think is best for you.

I wish you all the best.

Printed in Great Britain
by Amazon